One Step Ahead

For Al Moresso,
good friend, classmate and
outstanding leader.

Art Novacek

(see page 41)

One Step Ahead

a memoir by

Arthur C. Novacek

*How one member of the Greatest Generation
coped with the Cold War and revolutionary
changes in global ocean shipping.*

Foreword by Jean Fitzgerald, Captain, USN (Ret.)

Pure Heart Press
Main Street Rag Publishing Company
Charlotte, NC

Cover Design & Manuscript Supervision by Summit Communications

Library of Congress Control Number: 2006903706

ISBN 1-59948-026-3

Produced in the United States of America

Pure Heart Press/
Main Street Rag Publishing Company
4416 Shea Lane
Charlotte, NC 28227
www.MainStreetRag.com

Contents

Acknowledgments

My thanks go to all of the individuals who form the human fabric of this story, without whom there would be no story. I would also like to express a special note of gratitude to my country for making it possible for me to attend a federal academy, and, through the G.I. Bill, attain a graduate degree; to my friend, Jean Fitzgerald, for his support and the long hours he devoted to editing the script; and to those closest to me who put up with my dogged pursuit of this new challenge called writing.

Foreword

One Step Ahead presents a sweeping overview of the American maritime industry through more than five decades of its most radical change, growth, and development. From his earliest days as a newly-minted graduate of the United States Merchant Marine Academy at Kings Point, New York, walking down the city's famed Steamship Row to his first job in the industry, that of a lowly "management trainee" at the dynamic and inventive Isbrandtsen Company, to his most recent position as President of Eller and Company, Art Novacek takes us on a personal tour of the one industry that is and always has been America's lifeline.

A key player in the container revolution that forever changed ocean commerce the world over, a father of the "landbridge" that moves seagoing containers across whole continents by rail, a creative and successful senior executive of the hundred-year-old Grace Line, Transamerican Trailer Transport (TTT), Seatrain Line, and Navieras de Puerto Rico, and the man who fearlessly headed up the Soviet Union's U.S. shipping agency during some of the coldest years of the Cold War, Art Novacek, like no one else of my acquaintance, takes us there and tells us what it was like.

Even though this memoir covers those fascinating years, *One Step Ahead* is no tedious work of history, for it is liberally flavored with personal anecdotes drawn from the author's years of international travel and meals, meetings, and hunting and fishing expeditions with friends, associates and customers in Europe, Latin America, Russia, and the Far East. While his is not a pen dipped in acid, he does not refrain from recounting the personal foibles and management failures that he witnessed over the decades of his career.

One Step Ahead is a book that has cried out to be written, addressed not only to the thousands of American men and women who serve, or have served, in our maritime trades, but also to the general reader, who, knowingly or not, has been served by the mariners, the ships, the seaports, the dockworkers, and the maritime companies and corporations that over the years have made up this nation's lifeline to the world. *One Step Ahead* is that rare memoir, personally interesting to a high degree and historically invaluable in its portrait of an industry of incalculable importance to us.

—Jean Fitzgerald, Captain, USN (Ret.)

Prologue

This book tells the story of my introduction and immersion into the world of international shipping. It covers a brief period in our nation's history during which a war was fought and won; when a man named Malcom McLean introduced what was to become known as "the container revolution," and when our country's social fabric was colored by a Cold War that commenced in 1947 and would not end until the collapse of the Soviet Union in 1991. It was during this timeframe that I took my first steps into the uncharted waters of maritime cargo shipping; worked for several American-flag steamship companies during their transitions from breakbulk to containerized freight operations; and forged unique and sometimes contentious relations with foreign-owned steamship lines, including those owned by the Soviet Union as well as the fledgling maritime entry belonging to the Puerto Rican government.

I believe I qualify as a member of the *greatest generation*, the term coined by Tom Brokaw for those who grew up during the Great Depression; made it through World War II; took advantage of the GI Bill to advance their education and guarantee their mortgages; started and raised large families; and worked long hours to achieve some measure of success. As a second generation American from a blue-collar family, born and raised in Omaha, which at that time still had a small-town atmosphere, I never for a moment dreamed that I would be able to move on to New York City and a career in global transportation. Joining the United States Merchant Marine Cadet Corps during World War II and serving in the U.S. Navy during the Korean War gave me opportunities I would never have otherwise enjoyed.

Writing about a period in my life that begins fifty-seven years ago is not an easy thing to do with any degree of accuracy. It's bound to reflect how I now view experiences that occurred in the distant past. That's the nature of memoirs. I have tried to be candid in my descriptions of the people who played some part in my business career, but realize that my impressions were influenced by events of that time. I have tried to be as accurate as possible in explaining the specifics of the businesses in which I was involved, and fortunately was able to refer to data I retained over the years. In the writing process, I thought that I might be able to glean some "nuggets" of wisdom to pass on to the reader, but decided that would be a bit presumptuous. If there is anything worth learning, I hope it may be reflected in the telling, and that the reader finds this story an interesting portrayal of those times, laced with steamship management lore, moments of frustration and triumph, and quantum leaps in shipping technology.

*   *   *   *

Chapter 1

ISBRANDTSEN

Bowling Green, looking North on Broadway, Isbrandtsen offices on the lower right at 26 Broadway

It was a Monday in early July of 1948. Emerging from the Bowling Green subway station, I found myself at the mouth of the canyon formed by the buildings lining lower Broadway. It was a hot day, even by New York City standards, and I was about to begin a career that would span more than fifty years. I could feel my adrenalin flowing as I strolled across the broad expanse of Bowling Green to the Isbrandtsen Company, Inc. offices at 26 Broadway. Across the street, I could see the headquarters of United States Lines and Moore-McCormack Lines, two of a number of American-owned steamship companies operating American-flag vessels. They were in the center of the city block known as Steamship Row, a name inherited from the tier of row houses which had surrounded Bowling Green a century earlier and long since replaced by the massive stone structure of the U.S. Customs House which, in turn, anchored blocks of skyscrapers that stretched the length of lower Broadway. (The first of the twin towers of the World Trade Center would not be completed until 1973.)

In addition to the steamship lines occupying Steamship Row, there was, scattered throughout adjacent streets, a network of foreign freight forwarders, import customs brokers, marine underwriters, admiralty lawyers, charter brokers, towing companies, and stevedores which had made New York a center of world trade.

I was awed by the scene around me. At twenty-one, I thought I knew something about ocean shipping, learned from my Merchant Marine Cadet Corps basic training, followed by a year at sea as a cadet midshipman, and two years at the United States Merchant Marine Academy at Kings Point. I figured that as a Kings Point graduate and a management trainee, my new job title, I would deserve some special consideration. But I was to learn otherwise on both counts.

During my final year at Kings Point, the most important task facing each of us in the graduating class was getting a job. Besides our Bachelor of Science degrees, we would graduate with Coast Guard-approved licenses as Third Mates or Third Engineers and commissions as ensigns in the United States Naval Reserve. A few in our class planned to continue their education at graduate schools and some would go into the military as junior officers. Most of us expected to find positions aboard American ships, which was, after all, the object of our training. But I was uncertain about what I wanted to do, and I wasn't thrilled at the prospect of a life at sea.

One evening, the entire regiment was gathered in the auditorium at Kings Point for a presentation of some kind. Although we were told that the speaker would be a maritime executive, most of us would have preferred staying in our rooms to study for exams. Soon the evening's speaker, Hans Isbrandtsen, was introduced. A tall, ruggedly handsome man, he strode back and forth on the stage like the Master on a ship's bridge, hands thrust into the square-cut pockets of his custom-made suit, speaking extemporaneously in a convincing and charismatic style, with a slight Scandinavian accent. To my surprise, he inspired us all with his vision of the potential he saw for the U.S. Merchant Marine.

Near the end of his presentation, Isbrandtsen announced that he was looking for three management trainees from our graduating class to participate in a new program that he was initiating for his company. I learned later that he came from a family of Danish seafarers, but, because his father had been lost at sea when Hans was very young, his mother had insisted that he start his career ashore in the Danish-style apprenticeship system. I assumed that perhaps it was with this in mind that he considered an apprenticeship program a good one for his company to adopt. At the time, Kings Point graduates who went directly to sea progressed through the officer ranks to Master or Chief Engineer, with some eventually coming ashore as Port Captains or Port Engineers, never having had apprenticeship training for executive positions in the commercial and financial sectors of the business.

Instinctively, I felt drawn to Isbrandtsen's proposal. The Academy was to appoint one of the three management trainees, and Isbrandtsen the remaining two. He personally interviewed all the applicants, of which I was one, and picked two, but not me, much to my chagrin. I worried for days why this leader of men couldn't see that I had the right stuff, but I became the Academy's appointee, an event that changed my life.

On that Monday morning, the three of us trainees from Kings Point, buoyed by one another's presence, passed through the entrance of No. 26 Broadway, crossed the spacious office floor past clerks shuffling manifests and bills-of-lading behind what looked like a ship's rail, and presented ourselves to Hans Isbrandtsen, almost hidden behind his ponderous roll-top desk in the far corner. There were no private offices. He seemed surprised to see us, quickly calling for his assistant (and secretary), Bob Connor, who had been charged with coordinating our training program. But before turning us over to Conner, he gave us an assignment, saying, "I have a copy of *A Message to Garcia* for each of you. I want you to read it and understand the point of this story." Written by Elbert Hubbard in 1899, the story was an exhortation to hard work, unquestioning obedience, and loyalty. I did read it that night, and, in my youthful enthusiasm, resolved that I would never disappoint Hans Isbrandtsen or any other business executive for whom I might work.

Isbrandtsen letterhead with logo

We were each assigned to a department in the company, reporting to managers who were completely unprepared for this latest of Isbrandtsen's innovations. On Tuesday, our second day with the company, Connor gathered us together and handed each of us a thick packet of programs listing the musical selections that would be played that noon at the day's free weekly band concert, which Isbrandtsen sponsored. This event, held on Bowling Green, attracted a crowd of office workers from the surrounding businesses during the lunch hour. "Boys," said Connor, "your job will be to circulate and distribute these programs." A slender, balding, nervous man, ever ready to jump to his boss's whims, Conner didn't seem embarrassed at all to assign us this lowly task.

At the concert, we tried to weave through the gathering crowd and distribute the programs without drawing attention to ourselves. But no such luck. "Hi Art, great to run into you," exclaimed one of my classmates whose ship was in New York Harbor. "Looks like your trainee job is paying some big dividends," he laughed. Thankfully we were never given that humbling task again. I often wondered if that was because Connor found out we had dumped our remaining programs into waste bins that lined Broadway. But that is not to say that we didn't attend later concerts ourselves. We regularly joined the noon-hour crowd that gathered each Tuesday during the summer months, taking our lunch break along with traders, office clerks, bankers and construction workers, all of us jammed onto bleachers assembled that morning especially for the event. The music was provided by Dr. Edwin Franko Goldman's Band, hired by Isbrandtsen. Marches, waltzes and popular tunes of the day were the fare. I recall "The Parade of the Wooden Soldiers," "The Glowworm," and various works of John Philip Sousa, Edward Elgar, and Johann Strauss.

As for the training program, it soon became obvious that it was a first-ever such endeavor for the expanding steamship company. World War II had ended only three years earlier, and it did not dawn on me until years later to marvel at how much Hans Isbrandtsen had accomplished since then in assembling a fleet of merchant ships that circled the globe. Isbrandtsen had come to the United States as a young man during World War I, representing various Danish shipping interests. He gained a wealth of experience between the two world wars, heading up the Isbrandtsen-Moller Company (founded in 1928), which represented the Moller shipping interests in the United States. During these years, his older cousin, Arnold Moller, was building what was to become Maersk Line, and, by the end of the century, the largest containership operator in the world. Shortly before World War II, Isbrandtsen founded Isbrandtsen Steamship Company, operating several old ships in the routes between North and South America that were not served by Maersk Line. When World II ended, he severed his ties with the Moller-Maersk group and launched his own global services.

*   *   *   *

(Wide World)

The *Flying Enterprise* being towed toward the safety of Falmouth, England. The destroyer *USS Willard Keith* and the French tug *Abeille 25* escort the listing craft, while the British tug *Turmoil* (not shown) is pulling against the angle of the freighter's list.

Hans Isbrandtsen, widely known as H.I., was an extraordinary man, a pioneering entrepreneur who almost single-handedly built a successful shipping empire in a highly competitive field, operating steamships in all parts of the world. He had a penchant for making the news, and the saga of the *Flying Enterprise*, an Isbrandtsen Line vessel, provides a good example. In late December, 1951, struggling through one of the worst storms on record in the North Atlantic, the ship was heavily battered, and listing some sixty degrees. Her Captain, Kurt Carlsen, would remain on board, alone, for twelve days in an effort to save her. Just minutes before she overturned and sank, Captain Carlsen was taken off the ship by a large seagoing tug that was standing by. Given the nickname "Stay Put" Carlsen, he and his exploit became a major news item for days in the global media.

ALBATROSS

January 1951

Volume 15   Number 1

Nationalism

National Pride is self, home and country. It is strength and commands respect.

The great debate in this Country centers on the question to arm and go all out for war, East and West, or to defend these shores and this hemisphere.

This is not partisanship; it is a grave question that only the citizens of these United States should decide. They do the fighting and make the supreme sacrifice. No man or party of men should gamble with our heritage, barter and trade with our life or death. The foreign and international influences have much to do with our policy or lack of policy.

Many in high places in the legal profession have built up confusions in the interests of their foreign clients to the detriment of this country and its citizens. Self-glorification and a fat fee has done much to confuse our national policies, and left us pro-this and pro-that. Americanism, Nationalism and National Pride lie dormant in fear of persecution by authority, fear of foreign and social recognition. We fear to be different from others. We lack intellectual and moral courage to declare ourselves.

The United Nations, a super-government, foisted upon us, has a mandate to deplete our resources, suck our strength and decide life or death of our people. We have been engineered into an inferiority complex of bowing to our wards and debtors. This lack of national pride was capitalized upon by a foreign directorate to furnish men, money and material to carry on a war to perpetuate foreign interest at the cost of our own possible destruction or deterioration.

The cry goes out that the United States is in peril and vulnerable. This is a reality. From the United Nations comes the plea we must not quit in Korea. Korea, the graveyard of the flower of our army. International leaders would risk an all-out war with Asia that they may survive at the cost of American life and treasure.

House Publication of
ISBRANDTSEN COMPANY, Inc.

*   *   *   *

H.I. would take on all comers to uphold the principles and practices of private enterprise, sending his vessels through the gunfire of an illegal blockade of mainland Chinese ports by Taiwanese Navy vessels and from time to time battling with the Departments of State, Defense, and Commerce. He created a very personal house organ, *The Albatross,* which had so many readers his competitors tried to advertise in it.

Anyone seriously interested in United States foreign policy, as well as in the principles of its foreign trade, should read this paper carefully and take note of its implications.

He also took out full-page newspaper advertisements to express his views; issued his own authoritarian reports ("White Papers") on various issues; refused government subsidies; defied international steamship line rate-making associations; and fought with labor leaders and Senate investigators.

Another vehicle for his forthright opinions was *The Albatross*. H.I. wrote most of the copy it contained and personally edited each issue. He published it at whim, and would sometimes neglect to mention the name of his company or what its business was. Another outlet for his artistic energies was window trimming. He had use of a small window pierced through the thick granite street-level wall of 26 Broadway and his window displays occasionally produced sidewalk traffic jams caused by fascinated viewers.

Window display designed by H.I. commenting on the volume of paperwork required by ship operations in 1951 vs. 1891 (from the January 1951 issue of THE ALBATROSS)

Hans Isbrandtsen, 1950

Besides his global fleet, he owned and managed a number of diverse interests and operations including a large stock farm, Antarctic whaling, and the construction of harbor piers. He traded in steel, coal, jute, sugar, rubber and coffee, and also had considerable success with his oil rigs in Texas. But, despite his many global ventures, at the Isbrandtsen Steamship Company, requisitions for lead pencils required his initials.

He was a patron of music, painting, and literature, and although he raced ocean-going yachts, he walked to work across the Brooklyn Bridge from his home in Brooklyn Heights, which he encouraged me to do after I moved to that same area. (I tried it once and arrived sweaty and late for work.) Since I was from Nebraska, which to him meant I was a farm boy, he insisted that I spend a weekend working with him on his stock farm at Bay Shore on the far end of Long Island. I arrived by train late on a Friday night, was picked up by his farm manager, another Dane, and put up in a guesthouse that reminded me of the cowboy bunkhouses I'd seen in the movies. The next day, H.I. arrived at the crack of dawn, and the two of us were soon working in a field, scattering cow manure. This went on all day with no rest period, except for a lunch of sandwiches on the spot, and little conversation. That evening, exhausted from the day's activities, we had a Saturday-night dinner of Black Angus steak; then it was off to bed. I couldn't wait to get away from there on Sunday, and never volunteered for a repeat performance, thus proving that not everyone from Nebraska wants to go back to the farm.

I had arrived in New York several days before the start of my management training program. Disembarking from the train at Grand Central Station, I eagerly looked forward to my new life in the big city. Within minutes, things began to look up. "Hi! Where are you from?" I asked. She was tall and pretty with honey-colored hair and faint freckles on otherwise classic features. Apparently she had come from Ohio to New York to pursue a modeling career, and now was standing directly in front of me as we waited to collect our baggage. She mentioned she would be staying at the Barbizon Hotel for Women. After some hemming and hawing on my part, I asked if I could give her a call sometime. She agreed, and it seemed to me a great way to start this new life. But I must have been in a dream world at that moment, so taken by her good looks. Only afterward would it dawn on me. There I was, with only a hundred dollars in my pocket, constituting most of my savings, about to start a job which paid a mere hundred and fifty dollars a month which somehow had to pay for everything I needed just to get by. I never made that call.

I was the first in my family to earn a college degree and the first to leave Nebraska, going to the Big Apple no less to seek my fame and fortune. I was also a first-generation American, my father and his eight brothers having emigrated from Czechoslovakia early in the century. I had been exposed to the vast expanse of Grand Central Station on previous occasions when going to and from Nebraska by rail while on vacation from Kings Point. But this time I was here to stay, disheveled from the long train trip, toting a battered canvas sea bag from my Cadet Midshipmen days stuffed with all my worldly possessions: underwear, socks, two long-sleeved shirts, two pairs of trousers, a sweater, and a winter jacket. I was wearing a worn brown tweed sport coat borrowed from my older brother, which along with the trousers constituted my entire business wardrobe.

I spent my first two days at the YMCA poring over the newspaper classified ads for rooms-to-rent. After making a dozen phone calls, I settled on a room in a row house close to La Guardia Airport and across from the Junction Boulevard subway station. The trip to the Isbrandtsen office at 26 Broadway proved to be a forty-five minute ride in a hot, stuffy, subway car. I soon discovered that the other two trainees from Kings Point had obtained lodgings at a place called Trinity House in Brooklyn Heights, with a subway station only a block away, and one stop from another subway station in lower Manhattan, only a hundred yards from the Isbrandtsen office. Brooklyn Heights is at the very tip of Brooklyn, with a commanding view of lower Manhattan, and is comprised largely of brownstones converted into apartments. It is connected to Manhattan by several subway lines that pass under New York Harbor, and the Brooklyn and the Williamsburg bridges.

Trinity House was a co-ed three-story boarding house sponsored by the Trinity Church just around the corner. Hans Isbrandtsen made regular contributions to the facility, and thus we three trainees had no difficulty being accepted there. Little did I know that my future bride was also a Trinity House resident. The women lived on one side of the building and the men on the other; the two sides separated by a wall, with individual staircases, common living and recreation rooms, and a cafeteria-style dining room in the basement. I was assigned a cot in the attic, but over three months worked my way down to the third floor where I shared a room with two other young men.

The mission of Trinity House was to provide a secure residence for newly-graduated college women and men for a limited time while they settled into their business or professional lives. Most moved to their own apartments within six months or so, but in the course of that brief limited time, thrown together with the opposite sex, also with college degrees and with similar backgrounds, a number met, fell in love (or thought they had) and were married. I must admit I was somewhat intimidated by the intelligent, well-educated women present, perhaps one of the earliest waves of career-oriented women in our country's history. Not having attended a co-educational college, I suffered from a streak of machismo, with young women being a species to be pursued on weekends. There were about fifteen women and as many men who were residents at any given time while I was there, and six couples from those two groups eventually were married. (This group of twelve included me.)

The days at Trinity House were routine: breakfast served between 7 and 8 a.m.; off to work, returning in the late afternoon or early evening for dinner between 6 and 7 p.m.; and after-dinner socializing in the lounge or the Ping-Pong room, where I met my future wife, Jeanette. (She thinks to this day that she was the better Ping-Pong player.)

Art at Jeanette's apartment in Brooklyn Heights; Jeanette with her roommate on the back patio; at the park -1950

After about six months, we three trainees found an apartment and, before the year was out, I moved into an apartment of my own. Well, maybe it was not exactly an apartment, but rather a small room with a narrow bed; a tiny, scarred wooden table and two wobbly chairs; a hot plate on a grimy tin counter; and a small refrigerator in the narrow corridor leading to the bathroom. There was no air-conditioning, and I remember oppressively hot nights with the room's one window open, a small fan blowing in my face, and my head propped on a pillow close to the windowsill. The neighborhood was deathly quiet at night. When I peered out the open window, the scene seemed more like a movie set, with brownstone buildings end-to-end on both sides of the street, and cars parked at irregular intervals along the curbs. Passenger automobiles were still in short supply in those early postwar years. My rent was $10 a week, about a quarter of my salary, since after my first six months on the job I received a raise to $200 a month. I began to spend more and more time with Jeanette, and "You again!" her roommate's looks would suggest as dinnertime grew close at her apartment, a block down the street on Columbia Heights. Jeanette and I would occasionally walk across the Brooklyn Bridge on a weekend, passing through various neighborhoods in lower Manhattan. She would sometimes ask, "Why don't we stop for a cup of coffee?" This was a reasonable request, but I had little money, sometimes not even the ten cents needed for coffee for two. Obviously, this was well before the days of Starbucks. The few times that I did treat, it was at a diner that served bitter coffee in thick white mugs.

Columbia Heights faced New York harbor, the buildings of lower Manhattan clearly visible from the walkway on top of the retaining wall that ran the width of the backyard of Jeanette's apartment building. It was really just a small grassy patio jammed between the back steps of the apartment and the wall, but we spent a lot of time there during the warm summer months. We would also climb the narrow pull-down stairwell that led to the roof, a black-tarred area with a forest of radio antennas, air vents, and chimneys, where we could bake in the sun. (I don't remember any suntan lotion.) Another pastime for us was the St. George movie theater, a six-block walk from the apartment. In those days there were still double features, and we sat in the first row of the balcony so Jeanette could smoke. The theater was part of the St. George Hotel which also had a large indoor swimming pool. Occasionally we would go there to take a swim. Rental bathing suits were included in the fee, although Jeanette claims she brought her own, and we swam on our backs so that we could see ourselves in the mirrored ceiling.

My Kings Point education and my Bachelor of Science degree were somewhat short on liberal arts, so I enrolled for a year of evening courses at Columbia University. The most interesting course I took there proved to be philosophy. Until then, I had had no idea that such a rich trove of thought existed, treasures found in the works of Socrates, Plato and Aristotle, and the wonders of reasoning, logic, inquiry, deduction and reflection they revealed. My only confidante on these newfound subjects was Jeanette, and I remember weekends when we lay side by side on a grassy slope in Brooklyn's Prospect Park while I read aloud from my textbooks. It was a welcome relief from the routine of day-to-day business.

My training at Isbrandtsen was confined mainly to the company's steamship liner business, the operation of cargo ships on regular routes serving ports on fixed schedules, and carrying general cargoes. At the time, Isbrandtsen operated thirteen vessels on a route that took them east around the world from New York, traversing the Atlantic Ocean, the Mediterranean Sea, the Red Sea, the Arabian Sea, the China Sea, the Pacific Ocean, the Panama Canal, the Gulf of Mexico, and the Caribbean back to New York, calling at dozens of ports.

At the end of the war, the U.S. Government had offered its surplus of cargo ships for sale to private ship operators. The ships were sold at low prices and there were lots of them. According to Gerald J. Fisher's *Statistical Summary of Shipbuilding under the U.S. Maritime Commission during World War II* (Government Printing Office, 1949), there were 2,708 Liberty Ships constructed during the war years. These were slow freighters with cruising speeds of eleven knots that, by 1944, were built in an average time of less than 100 days. They were cost-effective, delivering supplies to our allies during the early years of the war and to our armed forces once we were part of the conflict. But before the development of the convoy system, in which dozens of freighters sailed in mass formations under the protection of destroyers, destroyer escorts, and frigates, Liberty Ships, with their minimal armament, were often sitting ducks for German submarines.

World War II Liberty Ship

It would be easy to compare Liberty Ships to throw-away cameras, inexpensive but able to accomplish their purpose, except that each Liberty Ship was crewed by about 50 vulnerable seamen. Few Americans today know that the death-rate in the U.S. Merchant Marine during World War II was greater than that of the Marine Corps, with a battle death rate of 3.898% out of the total number serving in the Merchant Marine, compared to a rate of 2,949% in the Marine Corps. (Source: *The Forgotten Heroes* by Brian Herbert.)

The Victory Ship was a significant improvement over the Liberty Ship. Although the deadweight tonnage (cargo carrying capacity expressed in long tons) of the two types was about the same, 10,734 tons for the Victory class versus 10,419 for the Liberty class, because of their better lines and improved propulsion machinery, Victory Ships had a rated speed of 16.5 knots compared to eleven knots for the Liberty Ships, according to *Ships for Victory* by Frederic C. Lane. I served on the *MESA VICTORY* as a cadet midshipman during the closing months of the war in the Pacific.

SS MESA VICTORY in port of Calcutta, India, 1945, to discharge 500 pound bombs (old box camera photo)

Isbrandtsen soon acquired ten C-1's and C-2's and three Victory ships. The C-types were designed before the war for a long-range ship replacement program, which was continued during the war, and were the U.S. Maritime Commission ideal of what they would like to build. There were three C-types, C1, C2, C3, the letter indicating that they were cargo ships and the number indicating the relative size. In addition to the "emergency," quickly-constructed, expendable Liberties and Victories, by 1946, more than 500 of the

C-types had been built. The C-2 freighters were 459 feet long, cruised at 15½ knots, and carried 9,074 deadweight tons of cargo. By January 1947, Isbrandtsen was able to extend his scheduled services globally.

The 1946 Merchant Marine Sales Act made surplus ships readily available to American owners. By the end of 1949, American shipping companies had purchased more than a thousand recently-built vessels (Source: *THE ABANDONED OCEAN* by Andrew Gibson and Arthur Donovan). Most of Isbrandtsen's vessels bore names made famous in the glory days of the great American Clipper ships just prior to the Civil War, such as *Flying Arrow, Flying Clipper, Flying Cloud, Flying Enterprise, Flying Independent,* and *Flying Trader.* Several were named for local areas, such as *Brooklyn Heights, Remsen Heights,* and *Columbia Heights,* and the *Sir John Franklin* was named for another famous ship. These vessels all sailed under the American Flag and under U.S. maritime law were given priority for the carriage of U.S. government military and aid cargoes, a valuable business advantage for their owners.

Isbrandtsen Line vessel FLYING INDEPENDENT (C-2 type) in Atlantic Service, 1951

At Isbrandtsen, some of my most interesting training took place on the piers where cargoes were stored for loading aboard ship or, after their discharge, were awaiting pickup. This was during the winter months, and I remember leaving Trinity House in the morning dressed in a black turtleneck sweater, an army surplus jacket, and a black wool watch cap pulled down over my ears. The first thing that I would see on arriving at the

North River Pier No. 14 was the "shape-up," at which longshoremen wanting work collected at the terminal entrance, where a representative of the International Longshoremens Association, the longshoremen's union, would select members for the "gangs" required by a given steamship line to work a particular vessel. No one today disputes the fact that at the time the Mafia controlled the New York waterfront. The longshoremen were a tough bunch and I would stand back on the fringe of the crowd trying to be as inconspicuous as possible. One day while I was working on a project that had me on the string piece, a 20- to 25-foot wide strip than ran the length of these old finger piers between the warehouse and the ship, I glanced down toward the water and saw the corpse of a man floating face up. His body was retrieved with a long grappling hook, and I was the only one there who seemed surprised by this sight. Of course, moviegoers reading the foregoing will be reminded of the Academy Award-winning movie, "On the Waterfront," which starred Marlon Brando in his first major role and paints a good picture of those days.

Hudson River Piers, looking north, 1955

At another stage in my management training, I was taken by subway from the main Isbrandtsen office to the North River for an introduction to Captain Sven Tang, a Dane, and the company terminal manager. H.I. had asked his son, Jakob, to accompany me, assuming, I suppose, that since Jakob was the heir apparent, his presence would be a good way for me to gain the attention of the taciturn Capt. Tang. Only 26, Jakob was a big man, like his father, with stiff blond hair, the same Danish blue eyes, and a pugnacious, unsmiling face. His father had declined to send him to college, arguing that Jakob was old enough to learn the steamship business, knowledge he would never acquire in college.

Jakob was shipped out on an Isbrandtsen freighter as an ordinary seaman. In 1944, at the age of twenty, Jakob left the freighter and enlisted in the Coast Guard, serving until the war ended. That morning, as we waited for the subway train to the North River, Jakob stood apart from me acting as though I didn't exist and not speaking a word. Once on the subway, I ventured a question, "Guess we get off in two stops?" Jakob finally spoke: "Yes."

My introduction to Captain Sven Tang was no more effusive. "This is Novacek, one of our trainees," Jakob announced. Tang, seated at his desk and buried in paper work, glanced up quickly and said "Good." I then stood in the back of Tang's shabby office, looking out of the filthy, tiny window trying to see the river while Tang and Jakob held a cryptic discussion. Finally Jakob left and Tang turned to me, asking, "How do you say your name?" After I responded, he said in a pained voice, "Well, I suppose you can research some of these cargo claims for me. Those people downtown don't seem to have anything better to do than pass their crap on down." Tang had a very pronounced Danish accent, by then familiar to me, a long, weary face with deep-set, bloodshot eyes and a grim mouth. He never smiled. I was told that he was very good at his job, but none of his knowledge was ever passed on to me.

I have long believed that Tang gave more than necessary attention to cargo claims because the claims department was under the direction of H.I.'s other son, Waldemar (Walter). Although Hans Isbrandtsen's obsession with business had given him little time for romance, he had paid suit to a Brooklyn widow, Gertrude Mirus, who was a switchboard operator in the St. George Hotel, the hotel with the movie theater and the indoor swimming pool. When the two were married in 1921, Gertrude had a five-year-old son, Walter. Jakob was born in 1922. (Source: "AMERICAN VIKING" by James Dugan). Unlike his treatment of Jakob, Isbrandtsen sent Walter to Kings Point, from which he graduated, actively sailing as a merchant marine officer during the war and earning his master's license before coming ashore to work for his father as vice-president of claims and claims prevention. But it was obvious to me that Jakob, as the successor to H.I. in the Isbrandtsen family bloodline, was the one H.I. had chosen to succeed him. Even so,

Walter was a pleasant, friendly, and hard-working executive, who seemed to do all he could to please his stepfather. Physically he resembled his mother, being of medium height and compact, with blond hair and Nordic features. He and his wife, Evelyn, became good friends of ours and Jeanette and I celebrated at least one New Year's Eve with them.

Pier 14 was one of a long line of finger piers that jutted out into the Hudson River. More than fifty years old, the pier featured a huge tin-roof shed which covered the thick, scarred wooden floor that ran the length of the pier, with berths on either side for cargo operations. Unlike cargo-handling facilities at European ports, there were no shore-side cranes for loading and discharging cargo. All freighters were self-sufficient, equipped with systems of booms and winches to move their cargoes, usually on pallets or in slings, between the holds of the vessel and the string piece of the pier, or to and from a place of rest in the warehouse. Cargo-handling hooks were very much in evidence as the longshoremen performed their tasks.

Most of my work on the pier consisted of digging through dusty files of stowage plans, cargo manifests and damage reports to investigate cargo claims. The key jobs on the piers were those of the stevedoring and terminal superintendents, several of whom were Kings Pointers and always responsive to my questions. Since my year at sea as a Cadet-Midshipman was spent on a Victory freighter, I had had ample opportunity to observe cargo handling in many ports as we made our way around the world in the closing weeks

All Isbrandtsen vessels on liner trade routes were self-loading, equipped with booms and winches.

of the war. Nothing had changed in the manner of loading and unloading general cargo. In fact, other than powered winches, nothing had changed in more than a thousand years. The typical freighter cargo operation, loading or unloading, could take a week or more. I recall that my ship, the *MESA VICTORY,* required ten days to discharge a cargo of 500-pound bombs and other war supplies in Calcutta and two weeks to load coffee in Santos, Brazil. But being self-contained did have some advantages. For example, we were able to discharge ammunition and other supplies onto lighters for the advancing U.S. Army while tied up alongside a sunken Japanese merchant ship in Manila Bay. Still, as later chapters will report, such methods of handling waterborne general cargoes were soon to experience revolutionary changes.

Since Capt. Tang barely noted my existence, I had to make my own way. Tang had excellent access to H.I., a fellow Dane, who occasionally came down to the pier, always without advance notice. On those occasions, I tried to make H.I aware of my presence by walking past him, carrying stacks of paper which I was intently scrutinizing. He would only nod to me, but that was better than nothing.

An enjoyable part of my days on the docks was lunchtime, when I would wander across the street to the Washington Fish Market, which doesn't exist anymore. I would walk down one lane after another looking at varieties of fish from all over the world, stacked neatly on display counters. But, with little money, I usually ended up eating a hot dog. It seemed that everyone made more money than I was making, including all those in the main office except the mail boy, all the longshoremen, all the seafarers aboard ship, and, no doubt, all the fishmongers at Washington Market. Still, from time to time I was able to earn some additional money by working as a "night mate," standing duty throughout the night on board Isbrandtsen vessels in place of regular ship's officers who were allowed time ashore. The only things I recall about that duty was enjoying the hours of dusk out on the deck of the silent ship, trying to stay awake, and fighting fatigue to get to the office on time in the morning.

My closest hands-on experience in handling cargo during my trainee period was occasioned by an Isbrandtsen run-in with the ILA, the powerful longshoremen's union. My recollection is that the union had called a wildcat strike of Isbrandtsen vessels in New York, and H.I. took the unprecedented step of mobilizing some of his able-bodied office staff to work a vessel that had been waiting to discharge cargo at Pier 14 for more than a week. He hired a large workboat to ferry several dozen of us across the harbor, from a berth in Brooklyn, to board the vessel from the waterside in order to avoid the picket line at the entrance to the pier. As one of the company's young bucks, I was down in the hold helping to throw bags of coffee onto pallets for discharge over the side to other office workers in the terminal. Even with some of our more experienced stevedoring superintendents manning the winches, it was still something of a Three Stooges movie scene in the hold, and it's a wonder someone didn't get killed. The funniest part of the day was when H.I. came down into the hold to act as our foreman, yelling orders like a ship's bosun. Our exciting experience made all the New York newspapers, but, thank God, it lasted only a day. I don't recall the outcome of the strike itself, but I certainly remember that my body ached all over the next morning.

When I was reassigned to work at the main office, I enjoyed my time in the vessel operating department where, each morning, I was given the task of positioning the tiny magnetic ship models on a giant Mercator chart/wall map of the world, reflecting the positions of the company's ships that were operating around the world. At times, Isbrandtsen operated as many as 125 ships, more than a hundred of which were chartered foreign-flag vessels (so-called tramp ships), operating on irregular schedules, and carrying full loads of various commodities. The others were American-Flag vessels operating on regularly scheduled liner routes. The chartering department was managed by Jakob Isbrandtsen, and its main objective was to match full cargoes (steel, grain, lumber, etc.) with vessels that might be available for charter. Depending on the nature of the cargoes in question, these could be single-voyage charters or time charters, a leasing contract with a stated duration.

As a management trainee, I sometimes thought of myself as a fly on the wall, observing all that occurred around me but not expected to make any decisions, or even being capable of doing so. Every morning while updating the ship position map, I could overhear discussions between H.I. and the operating manager, a young Greek captain, regarding schedule changes that might be warranted by operating problems. For example, too many liner ships attempting to berth at a given port could slow down the operation of all of them. Sometimes a decision would be made to bypass a port, or several ports, thereby doubling up the cargoes for the next vessel. These were all decisions made on the spot by H.I., a product of his many years of experience, but to me, his quick and effective decisions seemed like pure magic.

There were other reasons for me, still in my first year at Isbrandtsen, to be thrilled. Chiang Kai-shek and his army had recently retreated from Mainland China to Taiwan and the U.S. had given Chiang several old U.S. Navy destroyer escorts and gunboats to use to protect his position there. In 1949, he deployed these ships to the mouth of the Yangtze River and announced a blockade of Shanghai to prevent merchant vessels from calling at what was by then a Communist-controlled city. While U.S. Secretary of State Dean Acheson declared that the United States did not recognize the blockade, H.I apparently sensed trouble for the *Flying Independent,* which was about to depart Hong Kong for Shanghai, and sought clarification of the situation in a telegraph to the Secretary of State, also copying his query to the Chief of Naval Operations. The Navy responded that while the United States did not recognize the blockade, no naval escorts would be provided to facilitate the ship's access to Shanghai. Even so, H.I. directed the *Flying Independent* to proceed, in effect to run the Nationalists' blockade. As the situation persisted, three more Isbrandtsen vessels ran the blockade.

The FLYING INDEPENDENT, shown here with a Taiwanese Navy Gunboat, would live up to her name by "running a blockade" in 1949.

Confrontations with the Nationalists' naval vessels were inevitable, and several of the Isbrandtsen ships came under fire. In protesting these actions, Isbrandtsen sent cables to the Nationalist Government on Taiwan and telegrams to various U.S. cabinet members, and took full-page advertisements in leading newspapers, expressing his protests. The State Department eventually prevailed on Chiang to desist, but not before the affair had created an enormous media and public reaction, most of it favorable to Isbrandtsen.

Though no one ever asked me for my opinion about all this, I was exposed every day to the exciting international drama unfolding while I diligently maintained the vessel position map. Further, I became something of a celebrity at Trinity House and was besieged with questions each night about these events. My dinner companions evidently worked for companies and in professions that didn't seem to generate any such excitement.

*   *   *   *

My one-year training program at Isbrandtsen included time in almost all the company's major departments. In a letter to Rear Admiral Gordon McClintock, Superintendent of the U.S. Merchant Marine Academy at Kings Point at the conclusion of my training, I stated, in part:

> *I can say that I never realized there was so much to learn and how short the period of a year can seem. I didn't have the opportunity to train in every department due to the shortness of time and the general set up of a concern such as Isbrandtsen. I met with a few minor and expected restraints, which I now consider all a part of my indoctrination into the business world. In all my life, I never realized what a complicated world that can be. Mr. Isbrandtsen was undoubtedly the most valuable ally not only for the time he devoted personally but for the opportunity he made possible, leaving for us the task of attainment.*

This was somewhat of a duplicitous letter, since I believed a copy might fall into H.I.'s hands. Actually, the company was not prepared for its first management-training program. Many department heads and their staffs were not happy to have an inexperienced and ill-informed trainee staring over their shoulders and eating up their time. The company had a reputation of running lean and mean and was short-staffed, paying lower salaries than the bulk of the industry and consequently experiencing a higher than normal turnover of personnel. There was no medical insurance coverage and no pension plan, although at my young age the importance of employee benefits never occurred to me. At the time I felt that I was indestructible and retirement wasn't even in my vocabulary. Rumor had it that H.I. had on occasion quietly paid large hospital bills for some of his employees, actions that reflected the caring side of his personality that was usually masked by his brusque, taciturn manner.

There was also no such thing as a year-end bonus, and H.I.'s idea of a Christmas party was to call all of us together at two o'clock on the afternoon of Christmas Eve day, to gather around tables of coffee and sandwiches, no alcohol, with H.I. giving a report on the state of the business, a report which would then lead him to whatever might cross his mind, ticking off his feelings about the government, rate-making steamship line "conferences," socialism, communism, laziness, smoking, and drinking. The highlight of the afternoon came when he personally handed each of us a carefully-wrapped package of perhaps five pounds of beefsteaks from his farm. Status in the company was reflected in the cut of meat you received, and in my case that first year I received a slab of flank steak, which may give you some idea of my position in the company hierarchy.

*   *   *   *

As my year of training came to a close, the time came for my first job assignment. I was the only one of the three original management trainees still employed by the company, and thus it was easier for Isbrandtsen to place me in a permanent position. The trainee whose marriage had inspired me to marry, as I will soon report, had decided to take his bride back to his hometown in Missouri, where he settled into a banking career. The third member of our group had decided he didn't like the uncertainties of the shipping business and had returned to *his* home state, Ohio, to become a high-school teacher of mathematics.

I was appointed manager of vessel disbursement accounts control, replacing a person about ten years my senior who left the department in complete disarray. He was a very likeable war veteran and a friend of H.I.'s assistant and secretary, Bob Conner, but had difficulty in organizing the seemingly endless stream of accounts that were received from Isbrandtsen agents abroad. The department's function was to review all expenses incurred by Isbrandtsen vessels while in ports anywhere in the world. I reorganized the department, establishing a staff consisting of two assistants, a secretary, and me. By that time, Isbrandtsen had moved a part of its office staff from 26 Broadway to the first floor at 42 Broadway, where I was provided space for our four desks and a number of filing cabinets. We maintained updated files sorted by port with tariffs for all port charges such as tugs, pilots, wharfage, dockage, line-handling, stevedoring and other expenses incurred during vessel calls.

I reported directly to Hans Isbrandtsen for liner vessel disbursements, and to Jakob for those of chartered vessels. After I reviewed each disbursement account submitted by our agents, and charged back to the agent those charges that I found inaccurate, incomplete, or inappropriate, I would initiate correspondence with the agent concerned. I was required to obtain initialed prior approval of such correspondence from either H.I. or Jakob, sometimes waiting several days as the stacks of unapproved accounts accumulated. Seeking such approvals could be contentious, especially with H.I., who would fire questions at me as though I was frivolously spending company money, and expecting me to know all the answers to his questions about operations and expenses at various world seaports. Nevertheless, at twenty-three, by far the youngest manager reporting to H.I., I had an exaggerated opinion of myself and my abilities. "I was ready for him today." I would exclaim to Jeanette. "He thought he had me until I pulled out the letter where I nailed the agent in Bangkok for billing us for a second tug we never used."

I would troop down Broadway from one office to the other, loaded down with a bundle of accounts, leaning into a chilling wind that would howl up Broadway in the late fall and winter months. H.I. had two desks at 26 Broadway, one on the Main Deck, as we called it, and the other on a balcony called the Bridge. A steel ship's ladder connected the Bridge to the Main Deck. I never knew what to expect when I was advised that H.I. could see me at a specific time. It was not unusual to have to wait, seated in a corner, while he chatted with one of his ship captains at the mandatory owner's meeting held just prior to the vessel's sailing from New York, a standard custom in Denmark, but one that I would later find rare in the United States. I was fascinated by H.I.'s personal filing system. He kept important papers in a wooden barrel behind his desk. His custom was to fasten associated papers together and toss them into the barrel. But when he couldn't fish out the papers he wanted from the barrel, he would storm down onto the Main Deck, loudly fulminating against filing systems in general, not his unique personal system.

*   *   *   *

My rather pleasant private life continued, albeit at modest levels, with Jeanette becoming a daily part of it. Our activities were still limited to walks and talks, the movies, some swimming, but never a restaurant meal. I usually dined alone in my tiny apartment, subsisting on warmed canned stew, hash and even Spam, taken from the shelf of supplies above my hotplate. After two of our friends from Trinity House were married, with a grand reception and dinner at the Plaza Hotel in New York following, an affair on which the bride's parents had spared no expense, it dawned on me that I'd better do something to ensure that my relationship with Jeanette would continue. Of course, the significance of the marriage of our friends didn't escape her, and there were some hints thrown my way. After I asked the young jeweler in a one-man shop in the corner of the lobby of our office building the cost of a wedding ring, I realized that for the first time in my life I would be forced to borrow money from my parents. Otherwise, there was no way I could have purchased a diamond ring remotely worthy of my future wife. So I borrowed the money and purchased a proper, suitable ring.

The historic Trinity Church, where Wall Street intersects Broadway, was not far from Jeanette's office in the New York Stock Exchange, where she was secretary to the personnel director. We sometimes met at the church for a brown-bag lunch, sitting on one of the benches scattered throughout the adjoining graveyard. Trinity Church is a historic landmark, known for its colonial-era graveyard and the tomb of Alexander Hamilton which lies there. I remember well the day that I proposed in the church. The church's interior always presented a hushed atmosphere to us, shut off from the din of the busy street intersection in front. It was no different that day, as we tried to get comfortable in one of the church's worn, hard oak pews, nor did Jeanette give any hint that perhaps a special event was about to occur. Perhaps she thought I was lost in prayer, sitting there with my eyes closed. Actually, I was in a state of wonderment as to the momentous step I was about to take. Finally I got to the point. I could barely hear myself whispering, "Do you think you might consider marrying me?" while popping open the small box containing the ring. For what seemed like an eternity, she didn't reply, perhaps considering the options of "Yes, I might consider it," or just a plain "Yes." Finally, she too got to the point. Her answer was "Yes," and we've been together ever since.

Lt.jg Art Novacek at sea for two years in the Korean Theatre, 1952-1954, Operations Officer, Navigator, and Communications Officer of a fleet tanker

I continued in my new position at Isbrandtsen for a year before receiving orders to report for Navy duty in January, 1952. This was at the height of the Korean War, and I left with no particular fanfare except for the good wishes of both Hans Isbrandtsen and his son, Jakob. H.I. sent me a note, care of my Omaha address, forwarding an extra paycheck for the year 1951, a total of

$500, a lot of money in those days. The Isbrandtsen Company regularly sent me 50% of my normal salary during my first six months of naval service, which was a complete surprise, and money badly needed at the time.

During those Navy years, I tried to keep abreast of events in the maritime industry by subscribing to the *Journal of Commerce*, a daily trade paper read religiously by the maritime community. It covered all aspects of international shipping in its two sections, with the steamship liner trades dominating the second. The problem was that I would receive a bundle of two or three weeks' issues forwarded to anticipated ports of call as far apart as Pearl Harbor, Kwajalein, Eniwetok, Kodiak Island off Alaska, and Pusan, in Korea. It was a chore to maintain some continuity of events occurring in my chosen field, never mind poring over page after page of news about matters that seemed so remote.

*   *   *   *

POSTSCRIPT

On May 13, 1953, during a flight from Japan, his plane stopped at Wake Island to refuel, and Hans Isbrandtsen decided to walk the mile to the main terminal. It was an extremely hot day. After leaving the terminal restaurant, he began the long walk back to the plane and collapsed under the control tower. He suffered a massive coronary attack and died on the operating table. It was at least his third coronary. On the Main Deck (first floor office) at 26 Broadway, the disaster bell, silent since the Flying Enterprise went down, rang for Hans Isbrandtsen. He was buried in the graveyard of a church in Dragor, Denmark, his birthplace.

(Sources: NEW YORK TIMES, May 15, 1953, and AMERICAN VIKING, by James Dugan)

Chapter 2

ISBRANDTSEN Round Two

Following my release from active Naval service, Jeanette, our infant son, Mark, and I arrived in New York City on February 20, 1954, having driven across the United States from Long Beach, with a stop-over in Omaha to visit family. Our blue 1953 Plymouth coupe, which I had purchased new for $2,000 while I was on Navy duty, had somehow managed the long transcontinental trip, putting to the test its 98-horsepower motor and second gear used to climb hills along the way. The car's entire rear seating area from the floorboard to the side windows served as a huge trunk stacked with our possessions, topped by a baby's mattress and the baby. The determined little Plymouth dipped into the Lincoln Tunnel, followed bumper-to-bumper morning traffic, and finally came up for air to compete with much larger vehicles, driven by experienced big-city drivers, as we nosed our way into the traffic bedlam of Midtown Manhattan.

We were hoping to find an apartment convenient for commuting to the Isbrandtsen office, preferably in our old stamping grounds, Brooklyn Heights, and anxious to avoid another night in a motel. Operating out of our car, with the newspaper "For Rent" section spread over the dashboard but without the luxury of time, we settled for a furnished apartment in the Bay Ridge section of Brooklyn. This turned out to be "railroad" style, at the basement level, the living room in front, the kitchen next in line, a bathroom, and finally a bedroom. The small front sidewalk-level windows allowed us a limited view of the feet and legs of passing pedestrians. Basement life not being to our taste, we soon moved across the Hudson to a four-room cottage in Scotch Plains, New Jersey, costing $10,000, no down payment required, and financed through a mortgage guaranteed by the G.I. Bill of Rights. This would be the first of four homes we would buy over the thirty years of this memoir.

*   *   *   *

As I walked into the Isbrandtsen Company office at 26 Broadway, I felt as though I had been away far longer than two years. I was no longer a trainee turned junior manager, but a family man who had served aboard a naval ship during a war. I had applied to three law schools and was accepted by two, but three years of law school would inflict new hardships on my little family. Jeanette and I thought long and hard about this, but in the end I decided that they had endured enough, moving four different times from one shabby apartment to another as they followed me during my naval service.

Arriving at Isbrandtsen's building, I walked past the same simulated ship's rail that that had greeted me when I first entered this office as a trainee six and a half years earlier. After asking where I could find Mr. Matthew Crinkley, I strolled through the warren of desks on that same open floor, where no one had a private office, and it then occurred to me. The supervisors and line managers I passed were probably wondering where I would fit into the organization. They greeted me cordially enough, but since I was a returning veteran of the Korean War and entitled by law to a management position (comparable to the one I held when I entered active military service) and the only Kings Point graduate among them, I might well be viewed as a job threat to some in the management ranks. The circumstances of my arrival were certainly different this time.

During my training year at Isbrandtsen, I had had no reason to develop a working relationship with Crinkley since I reported directly to Hans Isbrandtsen, but I knew that Crinkley enjoyed Hans Isbrandtsen's respect and trust. With H.I. dead, I had lost my mentor, and his son, Jakob, who had succeeded his father, was a remote figure with whom I had few ties. Thankfully, Crinkley stepped into the mentor role, not by choice, but because he was the one I had turned to while still in the Navy, writing to him about the wisdom of returning to Isbrandtsen upon my release. While the company was required to re-employ me after my active military service was completed, I would not have returned unless I was certain that I would be welcomed back. While still on Navy duty, I had taken the opportunity, during a layover of my ship at our homeport of Long Beach, to visit the Isbrandtsen Los Angeles branch office, where an unexpected offer to join the staff came from the local manager. I included this in my letter to Crinkley, who responded, "I strongly suggest you return. We need you. The opportunities are here."

So there I was on my first day back, approaching Crinkley's imposing desk at the very rear of the office space previously occupied by Hans Isbrandtsen, behind a neat row of occupied desks. Jakob Isbrandtsen had chosen to establish his office on the balcony, known as the Bridge. Matthew Crinkley was a big man, over six feet tall, weighing nearly 250 pounds, with thick silvery hair, a large head, a pale complexion, and alert blue eyes. I knew he had joined the company in the mid-1930s and was approaching age 60. I also knew that he had previously been the traffic manager of a large tobacco company in South Carolina, and had met Hans Isbrandtsen in the regular course of conducting the leaf-tobacco export business. Crinkley was so impressed with H.I. that he asked if he could come work for him. Getting no response from H.I., Crinkley continued to phone and write, and finally showed up in H.I.'s office unannounced, almost literally forcing H.I. to hire him. Because of his excellent contacts in the tobacco export trades, he was appointed a vice-president in the Freight Department, gaining H.I.'s confidence as he applied his extensive experience in global commerce to the steamship liner freight business. He was now executive vice president, responsible for all freight and commercial activities for the liner services of Isbrandtsen Steamship Company.

Crinkley greeted me in his deep rumbling voice and with his pronounced Southern accent, directed me to a worn wooden chair alongside his desk. He immediately put me at ease, questioning me about my Navy experience and then regaling me with accounts of recent events at the company. It was as though we were chatting in the parlor of his home. At last he eased into the subject foremost in my mind, saying, "I plan to start you as my assistant until we can find you a suitable position." A company-wide announcement followed the next day:

> *This is to advise that effective Tuesday, February 23, 1954, Mr. A.C. Novacek was appointed to work as my assistant. Your usual good cooperation with him in that capacity is required and will be appreciated.* (Signed) *M.S. Crinkley, Executive Vice President*

Crinkley hadn't had an assistant, so I figured he probably didn't know what else to do with me. He suggested that I read his files to better understand the role he played in the management of the company. In turn, I suggested that I open his mail and answer, over his signature, any letters I thought I could handle. Thus, I had the opportunity to learn first hand the nature of the many sensitive matters he addressed as head of the Freight Department, matters that arrived from corporate headquarters, all U.S. branch offices and domestic agents, and all of our foreign agents. As I settled into my new job, we had lengthy discussions centering on important company issues. In the course of his work, Crinkley received mail from all over the world, and a side-benefit of my job was that I was allowed to keep the foreign stamps, which I did, and which I still have.

At the time, Isbrandtsen Steamship Company operated an "Around the World" service, a North European service, one service to the Mediterranean, one service to Puerto Rico, one service to Bermuda, and a service from U.S. Gulf ports to Europe. All but the U.S. Gulf and Bermuda services employed America-Flag vessels. Excepting Puerto Rico, considered a U.S. domestic trade, these foreign trade lanes were also served by foreign and American-Flag lines joined together in steamship "conferences," a form of collective operation permitted by U.S. shipping law. Conferences, with agreements filed and approved by the Federal Maritime Commission (FMC), were allowed to meet and set freight rates in a common tariff, utilizing a system of dual-rates, also filed with the FMC. Those shippers (the persons or companies who supplied or owned the commodities that were shipped) who signed conference contracts enjoyed freight rates ten percent below the standard rates in the dual-rate system. But Isbrandtsen refused to join these groups, and instead offered its own tariffs, with rates usually ranging from five to ten percent below the lowest conference levels. Most shippers, however, were signatories to conference contracts because the sheer number of steamship lines in each conference assured more frequent sailings and a greater breadth of port coverage.

The challenge to Isbrandtsen was to find ways for shippers to circumvent conference contracts in order to take advantage of the company's lower rates, and at the same time, defend the company's "non-conference" rates and independent services as being the better choice since the company did not participate in what Isbrandtsen viewed as the flagrant monopolistic practices of the conferences. This daunting task fell to Matthew Crinkley, with the assistance of a well-known former Congressman and attorney, John J. O'Connor, who was based in Washington, D.C. O'Connor was an imposing presence who reminded me of William Jennings Bryant, the turn-of-the-century politician, orator, lawyer, and statesman. While a representative in Congress, he had been chairman of the powerful House Rules Committee. When President Roosevelt used his personal influence to purge O'Connor in the 1938 Democratic primaries in New York, Hans Isbrandtsen retained him as Washington counsel.

The combination of Crinkley, the eloquent Southerner, and O'Connor, the politically influential New Yorker, proved quite effective in representing Isbrandtsen's interests in the Washington regulatory arena. The attempts by rate-making steamship conferences to compel shippers to confine their cargoes to conference lines continued to be targets of Isbrandtsen legal actions before

NEW YORK, WEDNESDAY, FEBRUARY 25, 1953

THE CONFERENCE CONSPIRACY

Recently, copies of a letter came into our hands which indicated eight (maybe more) of the larger American conference steamship lines, all heavily subsidized from your and our taxes, are conspiring, by agreement, to bring about concerted actions by all the conferences and their members to destroy independent competition on American foreign trade routes.

They speak of inducing our maritime authorities to order all independent carriers to charge whatever rates are quoted by the conference groups— (Whoever claims that conference rates are necessarily, or even customarily, fair and reasonable?)—or perhaps to order the independent carriers to maintain without change their rates for, say, one year, which would presumably open an easy way for the conferences to destroy the independents.

This conference crowd bewails the fact that their two-rate contract scheme is on the skids, and even worse, that the U.S. Departments of Justice and Agriculture are appearing before the courts and our maritime authorities in opposition to this monopolistic and unlawful practice

We noted with complete agreement a quote from a Shipping Board decision that

"The duty which the law places upon every common carrier to serve all members of the public upon equal terms has been evaded by many carriers subject to the Department's (Commerce) jurisdiction."

Boy, page the exclusive patronage conference contract two-rate system!

These conference people wistfully babble of legislation to make their monopoly secure, giving never a thought that, though their unlawful two-rate contract system will apparently be banned, they still can huddle under the umbrella of exemption from criminal prosecution for doing many things, by collusion, which are not allowed any other American industry not subject to total governmental control of rates or prices.

Every word the conference crowd say — every thought they express — every action they plan — is aimed at the destruction and prevention of independent steamship operations under the American competitive free enterprise system. Do you need three guesses as to who would eventually dance to their call and pay the bills of the "Society for the Preservation of Steamship Cartels?"

In our attempt to preserve real competition in ocean shipping, and protection of the shippers' free choice to ship with us—other independents— or conference lines, we have been compelled to carry the fight on the exclusive patronage conference contract two-rate system to the conference crowd. One certainty on which they can safely rely is that we have yet to run from a fight.

We have exposed this conspiracy to the proper Governmental authorities for their attention and action — but doubtless you, the freight payers, will yourselves want to take steps to protect your own interests. Upon inquiry we will be pleased to suggest the different governmental authorities with whom you might communicate in this connection.

ISBRANDTSEN

26 Broadway

the Federal Maritime Commission, in the courts and even before the Interstate Commerce Commission. As a result, Isbrandtsen Steamship Company remained a constant opponent of the conference system while continuing to develop and expand its own independent liner services.

In addition to cargoes generated by its aggressive pricing policies and ever improving quality of services, substantial cargoes were also available to Isbrandtsen in U.S. military and foreign-aid cargo movements which, at that time, were required by law to be shipped on American-flag vessels, and were not subject to conference contracts. Isbrandtsen enjoyed a large share of such cargoes; moreover, by generating its own shipments as a commodities trader, the company had developed another important source of business. But by 1954 the situation had begun to change, not only because post-World War II and Korean War shipping volumes were dwindling, but also because, like most steamship lines at the time, Isbrandtsen had failed to develop a marketing and sales program. This proved to be a serious lapse, and dealing with it was to help fashion my future.

By turning to Matthew Crinkley for guidance, I was well aware that I was shifting my career direction within the company from the financial to the commercial, as then represented by the freight department in a steamship organization. I felt that the work of the Isbrandtsen Freight Department in securing cargoes was the engine that drove the company and shaped its future. Further, the work was more interesting and better-paid and as close to a marketing and sales operation as a steamship liner company of that period could get.

The company's deficiencies in marketing soon became evident when several freighters scheduled to sail in the near future were seriously under-booked with cargoes. As a result, a special meeting of the company's key freight managers was held around the long, hexagonal, stand-up conference table in the back of the office, not far from Crinkley's desk and mine. (I was now working at a desk directly in front of him.) Crinkley chaired the meeting and brought me along, beginning the meeting with a simple question: "Well gentlemen, what are you doing to get the cargoes we need?" But the company had no sales department or records identifying key exporters and importers and thus no one present could give him an acceptable answer. The company relied solely on direct relations with a handful of major freight forwarders, companies that handled all the details and paperwork in booking and moving cargo by ocean carriers, acting as agents on behalf of the shippers. Their influence over the routing of cargoes had begun to shrink as the major exporters and importers recognized the value of directly selecting the carriers for their cargoes, thus giving them more leverage in negotiating freight rates.

The need for a marketing and sales department had finally been recognized at Isbrandtsen. In a matter of days, with some prompting from me, Crinkley determined that an active sales program was essential to the continued growth of the company. Henry Betjemann, a long time Isbrandtsen employee and the manager of the Philadelphia office, was moved to New York as vice-president of freight sales, and I was appointed his assistant. At last, a suitable position had been created for me. We set up shop in a far corner of the main floor, our desks facing and abutting each other, and, like stepchildren, were grudgingly tolerated by the old-line freight managers. Henry was tall, lean, and good-natured, a Jimmy Stewart type, likely chosen for this new position in some measure because of those traits, and also because he had a good relationship with the manager of the freight traffic department with whom he would have to interface on a daily basis, and to whom our new department posed a threat. Betjemann had performed well in Philadelphia with its limited market, but was ill-prepared for formulating a comprehensive marketing and sales plan for the company's liner services. That's where I came in, and this new job fitted in well with my decision to earn a graduate degree, specializing in marketing. In short order, we moved ahead, adding a secretary and four salesmen to our small department.

With my job firmly established, I applied to the New York University Graduate School of Business Administration, under the Korean War version of the G.I. Bill, receiving $80 a month from the Veterans Administration with which I paid my tuition and purchased my books and school supplies.

Isbrandtsen Freight Salesmen Alan Gray and George Rodgers with Art

I was admitted for the fall term on July 20, 1954. The school was at 90 Trinity Place in an old building downtown, just a few blocks from my office, with classes from 6:00 p.m. to 9:00 p.m., three nights a week.

Most of the students in these evening sessions were, like me, veterans who worked full-time, and all took their studies seriously. On class nights, I usually didn't get home until after eleven o'clock, but my studies blended well with my new position at work. One of my first courses was "Marketing, Principles & Practices," which confirmed at the first session of the class that every business must identify its market.

Art sitting on his desk in the sales department at Isbrandtsen in late 1954. Note large fan in rear. (There was no air conditioning.)

Acting on that simple precept, we realized that our first challenge was to identify our customers – current and potential. We set up records for our current customers, since that information was readily available in our cargo manifests. But, although the United States Customs Department required that all ship manifests be filed with them, this information was not available to the public. I soon learned, however, that cargo manifests for our competitors could be purchased at many of our foreign ports of call, where customs employees were perhaps not so scrupulous about the rules. To organize the information we were collecting, I designed a large, pre-printed form, one for every shipper of record, on which all shipments from these manifests, including the name of the steamship line used, commodities shipped, to whom, and the quantity, were manually recorded. I hired two clerks to perform this work. Interestingly, in recent years, a company has been established which has gained access to customs records and routinely provides all such data to its customers, priced according to how much data is needed.

But in those early days we were also obliged to determine the addresses of this growing list of potential customers in order to establish sales territories for each of our four freight salesmen. (Downtown, Midtown and Uptown Manhattan, for example.) Steamship line cargo salesmen at that time were called "solicitors," the thinking being that the term salesmen" could apply only to those who were actually *selling* a product, like a vacuum cleaner, not a service, like space on a ship sailing to, say, Bombay.

Isbrandtsen branch offices, as well as domestic and foreign agents, in time, added sales departments. Today, it's hard to believe that we were among the pioneers in establishing a function that is considered so basic to any business. Modern steamship carriers have worldwide sales departments whose staffs may number over a thousand sales persons. Without e-mail, and with the high cost of cables and faxes in those days, I designed a flimsy paper form that was used in duplicate, the top half to report the results of each sales call. A copy of the form was mailed to our foreign agent, requiring him to make a sales call on the consignee (buyer) to attempt to secure routing instructions to the supplier favorable to our company. The bottom half of the form was used to report our agent's results to us.

As we slowly developed a sales plan I handled the paperwork and provided most of the direction of the new sales force, with Henry Betjemann sitting across from me, uninterested in such detail. I was distressed that he rarely made sales calls. I thought it obvious that the vice-president of sales be involved with our major accounts, but often had to beg him to join in our work. He had the personality and the knowledge, but not the drive. On the other hand, reflecting back on the situation, I had never made a sales call in my life, so who was I to complain? But that was to change. Even though Isbrandtsen generally quoted the lowest freight rates, it took salesmanship to persuade a customer to cancel or circumvent his conference contract and ship with us.

Shipments were usually made on a C.I.F. (cost, insurance, freight) basis, with the shipper having the legal right to select the ocean carrier, or on a F.O.B. (free-on-board) basis, with the consignee entitled to make that decision. We therefore had to convince the shipper that he could have his cake and eat it too by asking his consignees to designate routing on an F.O.B. basis to take advantage of our lower freight rates, or to use a C.I.F basis if for some reason Isbrandtsen was unable to provide the fastest or most direct service. Thereby the shipper was not subject to the penalties that could be imposed under the terms of a conference contract. We obtained an authoritative textbook that defined these terms, and provided excerpts to interested shippers to make them comfortable in following our suggestion.

I continued in my position until June 1957, becoming increasingly bored and anxious for a new challenge, which didn't seem possible with Henry Betjemann having shown no sign of planning to retire. The nature of my work, however, fit in neatly with my studies at NYU. I was able to use my workday experiences on many of my school assignments, and spent most of my lunch hours completing my homework on an office typewriter. It was difficult to develop personal relationships with the Freight Department staff, since the twenty or so employees in the Bill-of-Lading section were all local New Yorkers who had no interest in advanced education, and the middle managers in the group were at least ten years my senior. Two of them, in fact, were decorated veterans of World War II. Ted DeSmedt, the Freight Traffic Manager, had spent years in a German prison camp after his plane was shot down, and Gordon Swensen, Ted's assistant, a survivor of Guadalcanal, still suffered attacks of malaria. And there were other World War II veterans in the company as well. (Bob Connor had served under General Patton.) Typically, none of them ever discussed their war experiences, at least not in my presence. Ted DeSmedt went on to become President of American Export Line, and Gordon Swensen headed up an innovative freight service, employing former Navy landing craft in services from Florida ports to various Caribbean destinations.

I did find a mentor of sorts in the person of one of our salesmen, George Rodgers, a gentlemanly father figure recently retired from a major steel exporting company where he had been general traffic manager. This is an important position in such a company, requiring much wining and dining by steamship lines soliciting business. He had been a good customer of Isbrandtsen, wanted to remain active, and therefore secured a job with us. He taught me much of what I know about dealing with customers, and a good deal about how international exporting worked. He was also very supportive of my decision to go to graduate school for my MBA.

About that time, Grace Line, the largest carrier in the South American trades, was going through reorganization of its management structure designed to take it from its hundred-year-old practices and traditions into the modern business world. The reorganization process included an executive training program, with the trainees required to have an MBA degree. The company's Controller, Ed Ory, who was a Kings Point graduate, administered the program. We met several times at Kings Point events and struck up a friendship. He proposed that I join Grace Line since he felt that while I hadn't completed my MBA, my experience would offset that requirement. He also knew that in a matter of months I would have my degree. He held out a glowing future for Grace Line, then part of the W.R. Grace conglomerate, and I decided that this looked like a more promising future than I could foresee at Isbrandtsen. So, on July 1, 1957, I tendered my resignation to Messrs. Betjemann and Crinkley and accepted employment at Grace Line, effective July 24.

Some pay stubs I have showed that I was making $700 a month at Isbrandtsen. Ed Ory had said my salary at Grace would be $800, not much by today's standards, but pretty good considering that at the time hotel rooms in New York could be had for fifteen dollars a night, the subway cost a nickel, milk was twenty cents a quart, and movies cost fifty cents. My decision to change jobs may seem strange, but Isbrandtsen was no longer the vibrant workplace it had been when H.I. was alive, and I was 30 and felt a need to fast-track my career.

My years at Isbrandtsen were like the beginning of the Great American Dream: A kid out of a Midwestern agricultural state manages, because of one war, to get a free education at a federal academy; has the opportunity to learn his trade at one of the most innovative steamship companies of the time; matures further while on active duty during another war, goes back to the same company where he changes career paths; uses the G.I. Bill of Rights to go to graduate school; and is ready and willing to move on to new challenges.

*   *   *   *

POSTSCRIPT

The March 15, 1972 issue of *FORBES* carried a headline, "The Fall of Jakob Isbrandtsen" with the subhead "American Export Lines is in ruins, its assets sadly depleted. Was it hanky-panky? Or did Jakob Isbrandtsen dream too big?" The article went on to say that at age 46, Jakob Isbrandtsen had been president of American Export Industries and worth at least $50 million, and that by age 50, he was out of the company, with most of his holdings in hock and earning a modest living as chairman of Manhattan's South Street Seaport Museum.

Chapter 3

GRACE LINE

"Looks like it's going to be another hot one," Al said when I joined him on the Westfield train platform that early morning in July. We were waiting for the 7:15 Jersey Central Railroad train for the beginning leg of our daily commute to downtown Manhattan. Although we were not usually very talkative at that time of day, I replied, "Yeah, but it's a pretty good day for starting my new job." Like most of the men around us, we each had a suit jacket slung over one arm, *The New York Times* tucked under the other, and a briefcase in hand. Al Morasso and I usually took the same train. He had aged a bit since our King's Point days, but was otherwise still the same, pleasant and soft-spoken. He was on his way to work for a ship operating and chartering company from which he would retire as a vice president some thirty years later.

Our train arrived, and we boarded the aged coach car, found a vacant, yellowed, wicker seat, and promptly opened the window, trying to get some breeze on the 45-minute ride to the ferry landing where we would board a ferry even more ancient than the rail car. Oval in shape and about 250 feet long, the ferry had ramps on both ends, a center drive-through section for autos, and large public rooms on both sides, with benches that ran the length of the hull. After a twenty-minute trip across the Hudson River to the ferry terminal in downtown Manhattan, the final leg of my journey was a 30-minute walk to Hanover Square, where Grace Line had its office, a walk 10 minutes longer than the one I had been making to the Isbrandtsen Steamship Company office at 26 Broadway. Hanover Square was another of the landmarks in the old business district, which stretched from the Staten Island Ferry landing to Chinatown. The fabled India House, flanked by the Grace Bank and the Grace Building that accommodated the corporate offices of Grace Line, anchored the west corner of the triangular square. The W.R. Grace enterprises had been based in Hanover Square for more than ninety years.

I had just returned from a family vacation in New Hampshire and was a bit anxious on reporting to Grace Line that first day, even though I thought the five-month familiarization period planned for me should be easy enough. Ed Ory greeted me in his glass-enclosed office at one end of the floor that housed the accounting department, saying, "Here's a copy of your schedule. It covers just about every department in the company." Ed was something of a prodigy, already the comptroller of a major shipping line, even though he was in the Kings Point class two years behind mine. He had been assigned the collateral duty of managing Grace Line's executive training program. After asking me to consider joining the company, he had arranged interviews for me with both the company's senior vice presidents as well as several lower-ranking vice presidents. I was given a few written tests, and within a day was offered a job with the company. The executives I dealt with appeared anxious for me to become part of their management team and certain that I would be fitted into an appropriate position upon completion of my orientation. It soon became clear to me that I was viewed as different from the other trainees, who had no previous experience in the maritime business and were destined for junior management roles.

My orientation moved me through various departments, meeting staff and familiarizing myself with Grace Line methods of operation as a major liner steamship company, one with far more extensive sailing patterns than those of the Isbrandtsen Line. For example, Grace sailed five ships a week from New York, one of them a large passenger/cargo liner, as compared to Isbrandtsen's sailing of a single freighter a week. Grace Line was a subsidiary of W.R. Grace and Company, which at the time was one of the most diversified corporations in the United States with significant interests in the chemical industry, including Dewey and Almy, Davidson Chemical, and Cryovac; numerous manufacturing and trading interests in South America; the Grace Bank on Hanover Square; the largest outdoor advertising company on the West Coast; and Griswold and Company, a major general insurance broker.

William Russell Grace, the founder, was born in Ireland in 1831. Twenty years later he moved with his family to Peru, entering the guano trade with the firm of Bryce Brothers and becoming a partner in 1854. He moved his operations to New York in 1866 and founded W.R. Grace & Company, Inc. The company prospered, mainly in trading with western South American countries, chartering sailing ships for this trade. Grace was elected mayor of New York City in 1880 and reelected in 1884. (Source: New Haven: *The Encyclopedia of New York City,* Yale University Press, 1991.)

Down Easter

At the time, the day of the spectacular but short-lived clipper ship was drawing to a close. Grace persuaded a leading Maine shipbuilding firm to build full-bodied ships with greater cargo capacity, and with as broad a spread of sails as the clippers. These vessels equaled the clipper's speeds on certain runs. "Down Easters," as they came to be known, had a greater cargo capacity, and could be manned with a crew of 24, compared with the 100-plus men in the crews of some of the larger clipper ships.

Within a few decades, steam-powered ships replaced these vessels. The first Grace-owned steamship, the *Coya,* had a gross capacity of 4,600 tons, twice the capacity the experts had said was feasible. (Source: *Journal of Commerce* article June 16, 1958) But these ships were successful, sailing "round-the-Horn" through the Strait of Magellan to ports on the western coast of South America as far north as Guayaquil. Over the years, as the Grace fleet expanded, ports in Venezuela, Colombia, Central America and the Caribbean were added, and when the Panama Canal opened in 1914, ports on the western coast of South America became readily accessible as well. All Grace vessels were U.S.-flagged, and beginning in 1912 included "Santa" in their names, e.g., *Santa Cruz, Santa Catalina, Santa Clara,* and *Santa Cecilia.*

When I joined the company in 1957, the founder's grandson, J. Peter Grace, was President of W. R. Grace & Co., the parent company, of which Grace Line was, as noted, a wholly-owned subsidiary. That year, Grace Line was adding two new passenger/cargo liners, the Santa *Rosa* and *Santa Paula*, to its fleet. By June, 1958, Grace Line's fleet comprised 33 ships, most of them C-Types built in the closing years of World War II.

SANTA ROSA, twin sister of Santa Paula, built by Newport News Shipbuilding Co., Virginia, is air-conditioned throughout.

This was the nature of the organization that I joined, and I hoped to make my employment at this long-established steamship line my career for the rest of my business life. At the time, Grace Line was in the midst of a total reorganization, having brought in a new president (Lewis Lapham) in 1955, charging him with bringing the old-line company into the modern business age. Major shake-ups in management were already underway, and I wasn't modest during my interviews, stating, "I feel qualified to head up the marketing department." The usual response to this bold assertion was, "Oh, but we have a highly qualified, Vice-President, Mike Diaz, running that department. He's only 37 years old."

During the first four months of my indoctrination, I moved from department to department, making worthwhile connections at the mid-management level. I was already familiar with the work involved in many of the departments, and made a point of comparing what I observed at Grace to similar operations at Isbrandtsen. Upon the completion of my training program, I presented a lengthy written critique and comparison of the two very different cultures and business practices.

Then the time arrived for my on-site orientation at Grace's operations in South America. Ed Ory complimented me on the successful completion of my stateside orientation as he handed me the itinerary for the South American trip, commenting with a wry smile, "It's too bad that it all happens over the Christmas and New Year's holidays." "Yeah," I thought to myself, "just wait until Jeanette hears the news." With three boys, and another child on the way, she was none too pleased with my pending absence. But I was elated at the opportunity to travel abroad, no matter when. At Isbrandtsen, only senior management had been allowed to travel outside the New York area.

While Jeanette was left behind with three small boys, and pregnant, I was off on a 46-day adventure, covering 21 cities and ports. I embarked on the *SS Santa Paula* on December 13, 1957, debarked at La Guaira, Venezuela, and then visited the fourteen designated cities and ports, traveling by plane and car. I returned on the *SS Santa Isabel*, boarding at Valparaiso and calling at the remaining seven ports of my orientation on the western coast of South America on the return voyage to New York.

Jeanette saved all the letters I mailed home during that period. Reading through them, I'm amazed at how excited I was with my first extended business trip. It's one thing to travel as a lowly cadet on a merchant ship, or as a junior officer on a naval vessel; and something else altogether to be received by the local managers of a major firm with a hundred years of business experience in every country on the northern and western coasts of South America. In the years that followed, I made many trips for Grace Line to these same countries, with such travel becoming rather routine. Some of my feelings about my first trip for Grace Line are expressed in those letters. For example, on December 28, I wrote from Bogotá (Colombia) about my time in Maracaibo (Venezuela):

On Christmas Eve, I had about 6 slugs at the hotel bar, watching people dance and have fun, and then figured the "hell with it" and retired to my room where I read about the dirtiest novel yet, "Peyton Place." However, while at the bar, I did talk to another fellow, and we became friendly and spent most of the next day together (Christmas day). He was Bob Darnell, a pitcher for the Brooklyn Dodgers, who manages Maracaibo's baseball team during the winter months. The next day, he introduced me to a half dozen major league stars. These guys were all of the big league teams. But you know how I follow baseball, so their names didn't mean much to me. I do remember some guy named Jimmy

Dykes from the White Sox. Wouldn't some baseball fan have been tickled to be in my shoes? The whole bunch of us sat around the hotel pool and talked and drank beer most of the afternoon.

Another letter, written while I was in Caracas, reflects my impressionable side:

At about 4 PM, I caught a taxi to the foot of the mountain range, on top of which is located the new ultra-modern Hotel Humboldt, accessible only by a ten-minute cable car ride, which swings hundreds of feet off the ground. The hotel itself is like a crystal shaft, enveloped in fog blanketing the mountaintop. Once inside, I found only a handful of people in its huge labyrinth of lounges and other public rooms, all of which on different levels were pierced by huge semi-circular girders, and a winding staircase. Wagnerian opera was playing in the background; and as I walked over thick carpets from one huge chamber, into another, it gave me an eerie feeling. It made me wonder that the cable car arrangement is guarded by shiny booted national police, and that the hotel had a network of impenetrable underground passages. The Humboldt Hotel not only appears to represent a pinnacle of Venezuela's newfound wealth from oil but also a possible retreat for its dictatorship (General Jimenez).

Pursuant to that letter, I wrote:

I trust you noted the current revolution in Venezuela, which started in Maraquay only a week after I was there.

Also in Venezuela, while in the port of La Guaira:

I was almost nabbed by the National Police when I went down into one hold and out a side port. And then tried to come back through another side port without my official shore pass on me. As soon as a ship ties up in a Venezuelan port (particularly a large passenger vessel), about 25 National Police board, shake the ship down, and station themselves at every exit (or entrance). They are well armed and wear high cavalry boots. On landing at the airport yesterday I found them all over. This is truly Fascist country.

This extended trip was not all fun and adventure. While I was treated well by all the Grace offices and agents, and exposed to most of the local operations, I do recall trying to sleep in a mosquito-infested room in a motel on the outskirts of Puerto Cabello, Venezuela; being awakened on New Year's Eve by the ear-splitting chimes of the huge bell in the tower of the Cathedral beside my hotel in time to watch a huge spider disappear over the window sill a few feet from my pillow; enjoying my departure day meal at a dockside restaurant in Valparaiso to be stricken with the so-called "Chileitis," a severe stomach disorder diagnosed by the ship's Purser as a common consequence of the use of human waste to fertilize vegetable fields in Chile; and being confined to my stateroom for the first three days of my return voyage while I recovered.

I recall returning by a scheduled Greyhound bus to my home in Scotch Plains, New Jersey, after disembarking from the *SS Santa Isabel* in New York on Tuesday, January 28, 1958. I was deposited in a foot of snow, seven blocks from my house, lugging two heavy suitcases and having to trudge my way home in the bitter cold, arriving at our doorstep exhausted. This was a far cry from my later years at Grace when I would have made that trip by limousine. The next day, I reported to the Grace office and learned of my assignment to a newly created position in the company. An article under the headline "Grace Announces New Appointments" appeared in the March 31, 1958 issue of the "Journal of Commerce" and reported in part:

> *Arthur C. Novacek will initiate a program of trade studies,*
> *market research, traffic reports, and cargo analysis leading*
> *to the inauguration of a trade development section.*

It was left to me to define what this meant and to determine how to make it happen. My new boss was Mike Diaz, Vice president of Freight Sales. I remember being assigned a desk outside his office, and being told by Mike, with a broad smile, "Go ahead. Don't ask me. You're the one with an MBA, and did the marketing at Isbrandtsen. Lay out your own program."

Mike Diaz was an ideal manager, possessed of extraordinary drive and charisma and a great sense of humor. He was the son of Manuel Diaz, a Spanish émigré and a partner in Garcia & Diaz, a successful U.S. ship agency that counted among its principals the Spanish Line, an important carrier at the time. Mike was stocky, strongly built, with dense black hair and expressive, dark brown eyes.

Grace already had a three-person marketing department in place, entering data from competitive companies' ship manifests secured through their agents abroad, just as we had done at Isbrandtsen. The company routinely distributed competitive comparison reports, a process simplified by the use of one of the first computers in the maritime industry. An object of great curiosity, this IBM monster occupied a glass-enclosed, temperature-controlled, 20x20-foot room, but had only a fraction of the capability that a laptop has today. With the computer's assistance, however, I was easily able to produce graphs illustrating Grace Line's share of the cargoes moving in each of its trade lanes compared to the shares of competitive carriers, and to provide similar data for every active cargo shipper, so that the sales force knew exactly the share of cargo allotted to Grace Line by each customer.

Grace Line had an advantage over its competitors, since W. R. Grace subsidiaries purchased goods from hundreds of suppliers and a central record was kept of the total dollar amount of purchases made from each vendor. A vice president was assigned full-time to liaise with each of the Grace subsidiaries to learn if any of the potential customers of that subsidiary were not purchasing from the subsidiary despite the fact that they were enjoying sales to other Grace companies. The vice president would then make contact with the offending firm at the highest management level to apply subtle pressure, like, "Hello Bob, you know that our company, W. R. Grace, bought $542,000 worth of widgets from your company last year. I understand that your firm is not routing any of your shipments to Chile via our affiliate, Grace Line. It would certainly be appreciated if you could give us some support." I believe this was called trade relations. Perhaps not technically legal, in most cases it worked. Of course, Grace Line had by far the most frequent service and also enjoyed large blocks of cargoes destined for W.R Grace subsidiaries. Consequently, Grace Line was the leading carrier in their trade lanes by a wide margin.

As for the "trade development" part of my job, this was a far more nebulous activity, and one never before recognized as a necessary function for a steamship company. It meant connecting U.S. importers and exporters with suppliers and buyers at either end of a trade lane to create cargo movements. I found that very few companies responded to our offer of help in developing overseas business, and our offices and agents abroad were not too enthusiastic about assisting in these endeavors because they didn't see much benefit in relation to the effort expended. I recall one time that an American importer was interested in securing a source for exotic seashells to sell to curio shops in the United States. Recognizing that Chile has a long coastline and thus should have plenty of seashells, I approached the Grace offices in Santiago and Valparaiso about this opportunity for new business. I am convinced that they were irritated by my inquiry, because they responded by sending me a full crate of large mollusk shells, evidently chosen for their compete lack of any aesthetic appeal.

*   *   *   *

This account of my early days at Grace Line makes my progress through the management ranks sound simple and logical, and in some ways it was. As so often is the case in life, timing was crucial. I joined the company at a time of internal organizational upheaval, concurrent with a fleet-replacement program that not only phased out the company's older vessels, replacing them with modern tonnage; but did so during a surge of nationalism in the South American nations served by the carrier, which was to have a direct bearing on the competition faced by Grace Line and the direction taken by its owners, W. R. Grace.

Grace Line's newly appointed president, Lewis A. Lapham, not a product of the company's traditional management group, nor even an experienced steamship executive, had brought with him the vanguard of his own management team, starting with a brilliant organizational innovator, Ted Westfall, one of the two senior vice presidents who had interviewed me in the hiring process. Westfall was about 35 and had no prior experience in shipping, although he projected enormous self-confidence.

At the time of my entry, there was a power struggle in play, principally between Westfall and the long established head of all of Grace Line's commercial activities, the other senior vice president who had interviewed me. This was Jim Magner, a dynamic leader, well known in the industry, and respected throughout the Grace Line management structure. But Westfall was Lapham's man, and Magner never had a chance in the uneven struggle. I never really got to know Magner, although I had met him during my employment interviews, and remember seeing him on a few other occasions. He was a big man, powerfully built and physically intimidating, with a reputation for business cunning and manipulation. By that time, he was in his early sixties, and was being forced into an untenable position, a senior executive stripped of his authority by Westfall who was directly charged with the reorganization process. Magner ended his career on a special assignment in Chile that involved the negotiation of a cargo-sharing agreement with the emerging new Chilean Steamship Line, an assignment which Westfall managed to prolong over many months, effectively exiling Magner from corporate headquarters, an exile that ended only when he suffered a stroke. I saw him when he visited the Grace Line offices many months later, a gaunt shadow of his former self, seated in a wheelchair with his left side paralyzed, painfully trying to speak, but without success. It seemed a sad ending to a remarkable career.

The department I headed was Ted Westfall's brainchild, and he occasionally asked for progress reports directly from me, sometimes coming up with simple and effective innovative suggestions. One of these was to identify large shippers who favored the competition and to formulate programs supported at all levels of Grace Line management, devising ways to achieve favorable routings. Apart from the "trade relations" mentioned earlier, this often involved special efforts with the buyers (receivers) in the destination countries, using sales executives who traveled abroad to particular areas where they had valuable personal relationships. An example of such a sales executive was Jacob (Jake) Jalil, a native of Ecuador, who had served as the country's Minister Plenipotentiary to the United Nations General Assembly. He was a graduate of Columbia University, and had many important connections in Ecuador. Other such sales executives were Norman Maxon, an old Grace Line hand, who had long-established business friendships in Venezuela, Curacao and Aruba; Russ Goode, formerly based in Bogotá as general manager for Grace Line agency activities in Colombia, and now based at headquarters, concentrating on Colombia; and Frank Gomez, who had powerful connections in Santo Domingo and Haiti.

Shortly after I joined the company, Wilfred J. McNeil, a former assistant secretary of defense and comptroller of the Department of Defense, who had a national reputation as a brilliant administrator, replaced Lapham as Grace Line President. There appeared to be no positive chemistry between the seasoned bureaucrat, McNeil, and Westfall, who was more of an innovator. At any rate, in a short time, both Westfall and several others of his team (including Ed Ory) departed the company, to be replaced by Harold (Hal) Logan, who had worked for McNeil in Washington as deputy comptroller and budget director of the Department of Defense. Logan was an Oklahoman, a graduate of Oklahoma State University, where he was a lineman for the football team. He had an MBA from Harvard, and was a Navy veteran. I remember him as a solid, even-handed manager, with an analytical mind. I developed an excellent working relationship with him and, in time, he became another of my mentors.

Conflicts within the company's senior management ranks continued, and in retrospect are difficult for me to recount with certainty. During my time at Grace Line, the principal characters in the drama were my boss, Mike Diaz; Andrew (Andy) Gibson, Vice president of Terminal and Cargo Operations; and Hal Logan. Warren G. Leback, another outstanding candidate for senior management, had left the company at just about the time of my arrival. He had started his career as a cadet with Grace Line in 1942, graduated from Kings Point in 1944, and rose to command a vessel before coming ashore in the 1950s. Like other gifted young and ambitious managers, he went on to hold senior executive positions with a number of leading steamship lines, including Sea-Land and Navieras de Puerto Rico, and served as U.S. maritime administrator in the period 1989-1993. Andy Gibson, poised and talented, a 1940 graduate of the Massachusetts Maritime Academy and master of a Liberty ship at age 22, and someone with whom I developed a lifetime friendship, was the next to leave. He went on to become U.S. maritime administrator (1969-1972) and later, president of Delta Steamship Line.

In an unbelievable move, McNeil replaced Gibson with Admiral Harry Hopwood, U.S. Navy, and a former commander of the Pacific Fleet. It resulted in bitter confrontations between Hopwood and Mike Diaz, who made no secret of his contempt for the officious former flag officer who had no experience in the complex nature of business on the waterfront, in particular our relations with the I.L.A., the longshoremen's union. McNeil had strong ties with his former Department of Defense colleagues; and so, again, it was a no-win situation, with Diaz leaving to assume the presidency of a small, privately- owned steamship line, West Coast Line, that competed with Grace Line for services to a number of ports on the western coast of South America. Diaz eventually went on to the become president of American Export Line, reporting to the line's new owner, Jakob Isbrandtsen, a principal subject in a preceding chapter.

With the exception of Warren Leback, these senior executives were brought in from outside Grace, and contributed to the management tangle complicated by a corps of Grace Line executives recruited during the 1930's from Ivy League and other New England colleges and universities, who had been assigned to training positions in the management ranks of Grace companies in South America, where they eventually rose to senior positions. Among these were Ernest Senn, a graduate of Williams College; James Hoyt, Yale University; Albert Wenzel, Princeton University; and Edward Meyer, also Yale University. By the time I arrived, they held various key positions in the company, having been brought to corporate headquarters to replace the remnants of Jim Magner's old guard. It would be fair to say that they carried on the day-to-day business while the prima donnas from the outside battled for the position of executive vice president and chief operating officer, with the hope of someday replacing Wilfred McNeil as president.

This was the stage upon which I entered as a bit player, destined to take a leading role as the management stars fell one by one from their lofty positions. In trying to present, as factually as I can, the series of events that occurred in the few short years that followed, I must admit that the story reads at best as creative non-fiction.

*   *   *   *

Before his departure in 1964, Mike Diaz moved from general freight sales manager to vice president of Grace Line's Caribbean Division, and I was named freight traffic manager of that same division. Management changes were still underway, and after Diaz left, I was named vice president of export freight sales and began to travel extensively on business in the U.S. and in South America.

In truth, I was a hard-driving young executive, not too patient or understanding of the

Wilfred McNeil, President; Ernie Senn, Sr. V.P., Art Novacek, V.P. Sales: retirement party for Norman Maxon, 1966

pressures I put on my subordinates and fellow workers. I recall when, as V.P. of sales at a meeting in Bogotá, Colombia, of sales managers from the cities of Bogotá, Medellin, Cartagena, Barranquilla, Cali, and Buenaventura, I overheard a question from one of them, "Is this guy nuts, calling a sales meeting for Sunday?" We had all arrived late on Friday and were attending a Saturday reception and dinner at the penthouse apartment of the President of Grace y Cia,

Colombia, which kept going until midnight, standard for Latin American countries. No one was pleased to face a 9 a.m. meeting the next morning. But it did strengthen my reputation as a no-nonsense manager.

I often made trips, both domestic and foreign, with the express purpose of calling on customers accompanied by the local sales manager, and would frequently include our overseas specialists, Jalil and Maxon, both

Art, V.P. Sales, speaking at Foreign Commerce Club of New York, May 1961

of whom reported to me in my new management position.

My visits to these countries usually included luncheon and dinner events. These made for long days, but were useful in learning local business practices and building good relations. The poorest of these countries was Haiti, which I particularly enjoyed visiting because of its friendly people. The Grace Line agent in Haiti, Nadal and Company, was owned by very wealthy brothers of French ancestry whose family had migrated to Haiti generations earlier, and who lived in grand mansions in the midst of extreme poverty. When a popular rebellion resulted in the overthrow of the dictator "Papa Doc" Duvalier, Grace Line had a contingency plan for extracting the entire Nadal family on one of the Grace ships that called Port-au-Prince on a weekly basis. The plan was never executed, because the two brothers, who were in France, simply extended their stay there while one of their sons remained behind to manage the businesses. Today that son, Jean Claude Nadal, is the family member running the Nadal interests in Haiti, which include the largest bank on the island.

Dinner in New York City with Haitian Agent: Art far left, Mrs. Jalil, Frank Palau, Jeannette, Jean Claude Nadal, Mrs. Palau, Jake Jalil, and Mrs. Nadal

At another time, I visited the Orinoco River basin in Venezuela, accompanied by one of our agency managers, to study the potential for direct ship calls there. Grace Line hoped to participate in the movement of equipment and supplies to the large aluminum companies that had established major bauxite operations in the region. The place was like a frontier town, set on the banks of the Orinoco River, surrounded by jungle on all sides. While strolling down a narrow street, the agent and I were approached by a thin, dark-featured man who offered to sell us a jaguar skin (this was, of course, strictly illegal), which, naturally, I bought. Shortly after bringing it home, and telling my children that I had shot the jaguar in the jungle, one of them brought it to a school "show and tell" and informed his classmates, "My dad shot this jaguar in the jungles of Venezuela." The next time I attended a parent-teacher meeting, the teacher inquired, "Mr. Novacek, how did you manage such an extraordinary feat, killing that jaguar?" I had no choice but to come clean, and the teacher's disapproving look only added to my mortification.

Art with the jaguar skin, vendor, and our agency manager; Orinoco River Basin, Venezuela

There are many other memories of my travels in the Caribbean and Latin America that will probably always be with me. Once, while I was in Aruba, sailing a Sunfish and not taking into account the strong offshore wind, I was nearly out of sight of land before the local coast guard sent a boat out to tow me back. On another occasion, visiting Barranquilla, Colombia, while fishing somewhere in the middle of the Magdalena River, which at its mouth is some two miles wide, our boat went aground. The boat belonged to John Lynch who was at the helm that day. Lynch was the operating manager in the Grace office in Barranquilla, and was one of the several managers who were introduced to the Grace organization in South America by way of a training program that placed them as boarding agents for vessels passing through the Panama Canal. "Don't worry," he said, "just jump over the side and push us off this damn sandbar," with an impish smile on his face. Nothing seemed to faze this product of the British Isles.

I recognized in Lynch the ability and drive necessary for senior management, and was instrumental in arranging his eventual move to the Grace Line headquarters office in New York. John was a graduate of a maritime officer training school in England, and had sailed for several years as a deck officer on British merchant vessels. He would later leave the company to move on to executive positions with several shipping lines based in Miami and eventually rose to President and CEO of Seaboard Marine Line, which provides extensive services in the Caribbean and Central America, as well as the West Coast of South America. Seaboard would become the largest user of the Port of Miami in terms of cargo moving through the port.

While visiting Cali, Colombia, I caught a severe case of some form of the flu that was raging in that dusty inland city. I spent a week in bed in a small local hotel, without air-conditioning, visited each day by a doctor who gave me a shot of penicillin that produced no noticeable results. I finally decided to fly to Bogotá, where a doctor there injected an antibiotic that did the job.

Arriving in Santiago, Chile, 1968, Douglas Gorman, Grace Line Agency Manager in Chile, and Art. At right, arriving Buenos Aires, May 1966 Jake Jalil and Art

While in Ciudad Trujillo, I lunched with the director of tourism for Santo Domingo, a brother-in-law of the dictator Trujillo, who assured me, "There will be no problem in bringing your passenger ships into our port since we have very stable government here." But then, after the first two port calls of the new Grace Line cargo/passenger liners *Santa Rosa* and *Santa Paula*, a rebellion toppled the government, prompting the United States to send in the Second Airborne Division to protect American citizens and property. This happened quite unexpectedly while Grace Line's vice president for passenger services was visiting Santo Domingo to arrange the promotion of the new services. He was staying at one of the city's large resort hotels when elements of the Second Airborne parachuted onto the hotel grounds, secured the hotel, and hustled the American guests off to the airport for immediate evacuation. (Our V.P. later complained that this military action had interrupted a romantic tryst in his hotel room.) Grace was able to resume service in a matter of weeks, since the new government, which was controlled by the Dominican Army, was strongly pro-American; and Grace, as the only American-Flag service to Santo Domingo (formerly Ciudad Trujillo), was selected for the delivery of the military and relief shipments that followed the American "friendly" invasion. Not for the first time, the U.S. merchant marine benefited from a revolution in a foreign country.

*   *   *   *

No business firm can expect to establish a perfect record in decision-making, particularly in businesses that are innovative and entrepreneurial. While I was the Grace Lines freight traffic manager for Caribbean services, with an office adjacent to that of Mike Diaz, I was able to observe a bad decision and its consequences at first hand. In 1959, the Saint Lawrence Seaway opened, providing a water route between the Atlantic Ocean and Great Lakes ports as far west as Lake Superior. Grace Line spent months planning a cargo service from the Great Lakes to Cuba, Haiti, Dominican Republic, Barbados, and ports in Venezuela and Colombia, hoping to provide U.S. Midwestern exporters a savings by avoiding the high inland costs of moving cargoes to East Coast ports for loading on traditional liner services.

What Grace failed to consider was that such voyages took an additional week to reach their destinations because of the substantial diversion required to call Great Lakes ports via the St. Lawrence Seaway Canal. Moreover, Grace soon learned that it could not persuade shippers to pay rates higher than those they were charged for cargo shipped from East Coast ports. The result was that while some exporters tried the service, whatever was saved in inland costs was more than offset by the longer transit times and from delays owing to frequent adverse weather conditions in the Great Lakes area. Grace

Line itself experienced significantly greater fuel and other vessel costs resulting from the two additional weeks in the round trip, a staggering negative that should have been obvious from the start. After two or three voyages with little cargo and monumental losses, the service was discontinued.

While that folly was unfolding, I occasionally got a look at its progress when a meeting with the Grace Line Midwest Manager, Ted Johnson, took place in Diaz's office. Based in Chicago, Johnson had been an all-American college football player and looked the part. A big man and light on his feet, he was a vocal proponent of the new service. He and Diaz would return well-lubricated from a lunch at the Whitehall Club, the favorite watering hole for the New York steamship industry, said to serve the biggest martinis in town, and I would hear, "Don't worry Mike, I'll get the cargo. We'll fill those suckers from day one." The two often visited Ted Westfall on the office's executive floor in the morning, giving him, it is safe to assume, the same sort of assurances. I still wonder, Whitehall Club martinis or not, how exuberance could have won out over simple arithmetic, particularly when Westfall was involved.

In 1957, Grace Line developed a plan to add Cuba to its southbound service. Months were spent engaging the services of a local agent, arranging dock space, and obtaining the necessary permits. Fulgencio Batista was then Cuba's president and dictator, and Grace's newly appointed agent in Cuba had excellent connections with the Batista government. Most companies doing business in Cuba did not believe Fidel Castro's revolution had any chance of success, and this was what Grace's agent also advised. We all know what actually happened. Castro's triumphant march into Havana in 1959 caused Grace to suspend their service plans, this time with no significant monetary losses. The agent, Frank Rovirosa, was compelled to close his business and move his agency and stevedoring operations to Miami, joining the many Cuban businessmen and professionals who fled their native land. Today, Rovirosa's sons, Frank Jr. and Jorge, operate this very successful Miami agency and stevedoring company.

In November, 1957, Grace Line took a daring step in an attempt to pioneer in the use of large metal containers for moving general cargo. At great expense, two of its C3 cargo vessels, *Santa Eliana* and *Santa Leonor,* were converted to full-service container ships, with gantry cranes running on rails the length of the main deck, so as not to be dependent on shore-side gantries, which, at the time, did not exist in South American ports. In January, 1960, the *Eliana* became the first full container ship to enter foreign trade when it sailed for La Guaira, Venezuela. (Source: *THE ABANDONED OCEAN* by Andrew Gibson and Arthur Donovan) The major obstacle to this new service was the resistance of the Venezuelan dockworkers' union, which correctly foresaw the tremendous loss of jobs that would result from the simplicity and efficiency of container operations. In company with its agents, Boulton & Cia, a powerful Venezuelan company involved in many businesses, Grace spent months laying the groundwork with the union and the government; but to no avail. When the first ship arrived, the workers went on strike, and the vessel lay idle at its berth for eleven months. The union was much too powerful for the Venezuelan government to oppose it or to intervene, although Grace urged the government to do so. Finally, an accommodation was reached with labor to work this one ship, with the understanding that such ships were not to return. Both vessels were eventually sold to Sea-Land, which successfully pioneered container ship service to Puerto Rico, a domestic U.S. trade, where the local labor union had agreements similar to those held by its parent union on the mainland. Many years later, the objections of Latin American labor unions were overcome, and today all major South American ports have developed container facilities with gantry cranes in operation.

Once again I had a front seat as a drama unfolded. Grace Line had a lead-time of two years to lay the groundwork in Venezuela to assure acceptance of these innovative vessels. Working directly for Mike Diaz, George Spiotta, a close friend and fellow Kings Pointer, was assigned the task and spent many weeks in LaGuaira. George was an experienced operating manager, bilingual and very personable, who developed a close relationship with the union in Venezuela, aided by the longtime Boulton agency manager there. I was present on many occasions when George reassured Mike about Grace Line's prospects, saying, "It's beginning to look good, and I think we'll be able to pull it off," or some such words. Somehow, Grace Line was committed, and had no choice but to go the route, a route that ended in failure.

In reviewing those days, it should be remembered that Grace Line, unlike my previous employer Isbrandtsen Steamship Company, was a subsidized carrier, as were most American-flag liner companies of that era, including United States Line, Moore-McCormack, American Export, American President, Pacific Far East, Lykes Brothers, and Farrell. Since the Civil War, American building and operating costs for ocean-going ships had been higher than foreign costs. The Merchant Marine Act of 1936 established a system of construction differential and operating differential subsidies, the differentials representing the differences between average American and average foreign shipbuilding and operating costs on trade routes essential to the foreign commerce of the U.S. The expectation was that the subsidy-favored carriers would provide regular, frequent, fast and dependable American-flag liner service. All the subsidized lines belonged to liner conferences which provided legal, agreed tariff rates among the lines operating on a given trade route. (Source: *HISTORY OF U.S. CARGO LINER SERVICE* by Douglas K. Fleming)

Grace Line had many advantages over its competitors, all foreign-flag, in marketing its services. For example, in the New York-New Jersey sales area, every Friday one of the big passenger/cargo ships, *SANTA ROSA* or *SANTA PAULA,* was in port, and special luncheons were arranged at least once a month, allowing freight salesmen to bring important customers on board these beautiful vessels for lunch and a tour of cargo handling and passenger facilities. Also, several times a year, our major customers would eagerly await festive dinner events on these vessels, and Grace Line's senior management, including the president, would attend. Most of the guests were accompanied by their wives or distaff friends, and the Grace Line wives brigade, including my wife, Jeanette, whose social skills were a major asset, would be present in force. Many of the important guests would sit at my table; and, as vice president of sales, I served as master-of-ceremonies, taking the microphone for extemporaneous remarks, usually well fortified with Scotch and water.

Customer dinner on board the SANTA ROSA: super hostess Jeanette in the middle, Art at far right

These days were probably the most enjoyable of my years at Grace Line, but I was suddenly faced with another career-impacting decision point, which I found very difficult. Still, in the end, on September 6, 1966, I informed my superiors at Grace Line that I was leaving to accept a position elsewhere. The following chapter describes the next step in my career, explains my reasons for leaving Grace Line, and recounts my experiences in heading up a new company with an entirely new concept of moving cargo on ships.

*   *   *   *

Chapter 4

TTT

We became acquainted at meetings of the American-flag steamship lines involved in the handling of military cargoes. Eric Holzer was the owner and President of American Union Transport Inc. (AUT), a major U.S.-based foreign freight forwarder and a major logistics provider for project cargoes. He was a short, balding, dapper man, soft-spoken and introspective. As one of those meetings adjourned, he took me aside and said in a confidential tone, "I have a proposition that you might find interesting." The year was 1966, and I was vice-president of freight sales at Grace Line. At lunch the next day, he explained that his company was partnering with the Sun shipyard in Pennsylvania to build the largest roll-on roll-off vessel in the world, and that the ship was to operate between New York and San Juan, Puerto Rico.

At the time, AUT operated a breakbulk steamship service to Puerto Rico, using several old American-flag World War II vessels. Holzer's partner in the new venture was Sun Shipbuilding & Dry Dock Company of Chester, Pennsylvania, which was managed by Paul Atkinson, its president. In a unique arrangement, Sun would design and build the vessel to meet Puerto Rican service requirements, and AUT would operate it. Some $25 million, a considerable sum in those days, was to be invested in the new ship and the huge moveable ramps and other shore facilities needed at both the U.S. and Puerto Rican ends of the run. The vessel, 700 feet in length, was designed to carry a wide range of highway trailers and vehicles, and was to be delivered by the end of the next year, 1967.

Holzer's approach to me came at a time when I felt that my further advancement at Grace Line would be slow, and besides, this new opportunity looked challenging. I was very interested, and the deal was sealed at a dinner meeting with Messrs. Holzer and Atkinson in Washington, D.C., on August 22, 1966. I gave notice to Grace Line on September 6, and started my new job later that month. Paul Atkinson, with whom I would establish a good relationship in the months to come, was about 45 years old, lean and agile, with thinning dark hair, carefully combed straight back to cover a growing bald spot. He was inquisitive and entrepreneurial, much more outgoing than Holzer; and, when he wanted to be, very persuasive.

My first order of business was setting up shop in an empty office several floors below the AUT offices in the Whitehall Building, at the southern tip of Manhattan. My windowless private enclosure at one end of the office was a far cry from the large corner office that had been mine at Grace Line. Our office furnishings consisted of some spare desks and file cabinets loaned to us by AUT. The one other employee was John Huntington, a retired Navy commander, whose last post was that of transportation officer of the Navy's Military Sea Transportation Service (MSTS), which was based at the Brooklyn Naval Shipyard. John was a bit shorter than I, with blond hair going gray, friendly, but possibly disappointed that he hadn't gotten the job I was filling. He had originally been hired by AUT to serve as their liaison with MSTS in procuring military cargoes destined for Puerto Rico, but he was now assigned to serve as my administrative assistant and office manager. As the only two staffers in the new venture, we worked very closely with each other.

The company had been named Transamerican Trailer Transport, Inc. (TTT). Eric Holzer was president, and I was appointed executive vice president and general manager. The new ship would be fitted with large side-ports to receive containers on chassis and also standard highway trailers. These would be driven from the pier up into the ship and down from the ship to the pier on large mobile pier-side ramps, one near the front of the ship, one amidships, and the third near the ship's stern. There were also ramps within the ship to permit movement of the chassis and trailers from one deck to another. At a cruising speed of twenty-five knots, this would be an unusually fast ship, permitting a round trip from New York to San Juan and back in a week, thus providing weekly service. It would be the only vessel of its type operating in the United States trades, domestic or foreign.

Holzer had asked me for a memorandum outlining my plans for overseeing the building of the vessel, its introduction into service, the staffing required, and how I planned to market the new product and service, but it was difficult to decide my priorities in building an organization from scratch with the relatively limited assets available. I was so engrossed in pondering the options that on several occasions, on my morning walk from the ferry landing to my office, I found myself at Hanover Square, where Grace Line was located, instead of at the Whitehall Building.

Artist's conception of first TTT roll-on/roll-off vessel

By law, the Commonwealth of Puerto Rico could be served only by U.S.-flagged and U.S-crewed vessels. At the time, Puerto Rico was serviced by various container ships carrying 20-, 35-, and 40-foot containers, stored one on top the other in cells on board the ship. The containers were moved on chassis and transported by over-the-road tractor-trailers, and cranes were required for loading and offloading them. These container ships were all more than 20 years old, with top speeds of seventeen knots or so, and they would be no match for the new vessel. The Ro-Ro ship we were building had an added advantage: in addition to marine containers on chassis, it could accommodate any over-the-road tractor-trailer. The drawback was that while the ship would be much larger than the conventional container ship, containers and trailers would be loaded with their chassis and wheels, thus requiring considerably more interior vessel space. Consequently, the ship's total cargo capacity was less than that of conventional container ships.

It was therefore essential to develop a marketing program aimed at securing higher-paying freight. This resulted in a four-part program. First, using available data, primarily vessel manifests procured by various means, all exporters and importers active in the Puerto Rican trade were identified. Second, a sales manager was hired and given the initial task of visiting the shippers, receivers, and freight forwarders that had been identified; after each call, he was to prepare a data card for the prospective account, listing the name, address, and telephone number, the commodities shipped, and their volume. Third, existing tariffs were analyzed to determined the current freight rates for every commodity identified. Finally, TTT's rates for all low-paying commodities were set at high levels designed to discourage their booking via our service.

"Hi Paul, this is Art Novacek, how about lunch?" As I cradled my phone, I reflected on the man I hoped to hire as sales manager, Paul Semack, in my opinion the most aggressive and innovative of Grace Line's salesmen. He accepted my invitation. Paul was about my age, strongly built and tough looking, with a ruddy complexion, good-humored and well liked. At one time in his life, Paul had sold home sidings -- not an easy sales job. I believed, correctly, that he would be eager to join me in this new venture. "Figure me on-board, Art," Paul said. "When do I start?" And so I hired my first employee. Paul eventually became vice president of sales for TTT.

I was to make many trips to Puerto Rico in the months to come. We had to start building an organization there, find office space, and plan for a terminal capable of meeting our roll-on roll-off berthing and terminal requirements. On my first visit to San Juan, I had a lucky encounter. As I was at the check-in counter of my hotel, I felt a tap on my shoulder and heard, "Hello, I'm Roberto Lugo, and I'm looking for a job." Lugo had been General Manager for Seatrain Line in Puerto Rico, but a serious clash of personalities with his superior in New Jersey led to his dismissal. After some discussion, I hired him as the

TTT General Manager for Puerto Rico, and thus began a friendship that has lasted until this day.

Lugo immediately set up a temporary office; made contact with the government officials running the Port of San Juan in order to commence negotiations for a terminal; appointed an agent for the ports of Ponce and Mayaguez; and worked with me on a marketing plan for Puerto Rico. We were in phone contact almost every day. Roberto was a year older than I, several inches shorter, with graying hair and a confident attitude. He was a C.P.A., well-educated, perceptive, a commissioned officer in the Puerto Rico National Guard, liked to play softball, and seemed to know just about everyone who counted in government or in business in Puerto Rico. He would play a very important role in my future, at a critical time for me.

Night Club in San Juan: at far left, Mrs. Lugo; right of center, Roberto, Art and Jeanette; 1966

We began an aggressive program to introduce our new service to government officials by hosting several lunches that helped lay the groundwork for our terminal needs. It was a tiring but also exhilarating time for me. During this period we attacked the customer base in the same fashion, being very visible at industry affairs. We were the talk of the shipping industry in Puerto Rico, and seemed to be making all the right moves.

Puerto Rico was the beneficiary of Operation Bootstrap, a U.S. government program that allowed mainland industries to establish and operate manufacturing facilities in Puerto Rico, free of federal taxes. Under the program, U.S. firms shipped raw and semi-finished materials to Puerto Rico for assembly or manufacture into finished products by their local subsidiaries, and return shipment to the mainland. The pharmaceutical, garment, and toiletry industries were among the largest participants in the program.

Addressing key Puerto Rican government officials and shippers in San Juan

Puerto Rico Manufacturers Association Convention, San Juan, November 1966. John Huntington far right, Art and Jeanette, third and fourth from right.

*   *   *   *

After my first few weeks on the job, Holzer said, "Art I think you should get some background as to how Ro-Ro operations are handled in the English 'short sea' trades." In reply, I asked, "What are they?" "Well, for some time there have been roll-on roll-off services connecting English ports with those on the Continent. They're called short sea, since it is such a short trip across the English Channel. There's a heavy equipment exhibition in two weeks in Southampton which will give you an opportunity to check on the types of equipment we may need. Also, there are Ro-Ro services operating out of Southampton to ports in France and Belgium, which you may be able to observe first-hand."

It was my first trip to Europe. Despite the fact that I had gone around the world as a cadet on a merchant ship, and seen much of South America during my indoctrination at Grace Line, visiting London and Paris was in a different travel league. After an overnight flight to London from New York, I went from Heathrow to my hotel by what to me was a quaint vehicle, a black London taxicab, indistinguishable from the hundreds of other cabs on the road. The hour-long cab ride gave me a wonderful opportunity to study the mixture of old and new architecture along the way, especially as we approached Mayfair and my hotel. I was entranced by block after block of white concrete three-and four-story hotels, with covered entrances and small markers bearing their names. In later years, I traversed this route many times, and it always gave me a comfortable feeling knowing that I would soon experience again the formalities of the English, at least the English in London. The next morning I found myself up at dawn, wandering the largely deserted streets on a Sunday morning, taking in those sights that so often awe first-time American visitors, such as Buckingham Palace and Westminster Cathedral. I even ordered smoked herring instead of bacon with my eggs for breakfast that morning, before boarding a tourist bus for the standard city tour, taking advantage of my first full day in the city.

The next morning, I taxied to Victoria Station, that vast cavern with its numerous boarding platforms that has served as the backdrop for so many British films, and managed to find my first-class coach and compartment on the train to Southampton. The train was old, but far more pleasant than the trains of the Jersey Central. I enjoyed the passing view of the English countryside, so different from the New Jersey I saw on my train rides to New York, manicured fields and small villages, not some sprawling New Jersey town abutting the next, and no room to catch your breath in between. I checked into my hotel in Southampton and then proceeded to the exhibition center.

I was soon making the rounds of the various exhibitors, looking mostly at heavy-duty terminal tractors and container handling equipment. Although worn from the trip, I tried my best to be gregarious, and soon found myself conversing with many of the exhibitors' representatives, asking questions and making some friends. That's when I was first exposed to the English caste system. At noon, "How about some lunch?" one of them asked, and off we went, three of us, to a local pub for a pint of "bitters" (warm beer) and sandwiches. These two men were sales managers for their companies, and spoke with intriguing regional accents.

It was an enjoyable luncheon, and not to be outdone, I asked, "How about joining me for dinner tonight? We can go to the dining room on the top floor of the hotel. I understand it has great food." Both of them looked at me as though I was a bit daft, as they would say. "We can't go to that place. That's where our bosses eat during the exhibition, and we don't mix socially outside the office." I asked why not and was told, "Apart from upper management, we also have upper classes, with long family lineages, which we take for granted. After all, these blokes do step forward when our islands are threatened, most as officer volunteers, and a great bunch of them died in the trenches in the Great War, and in the fighting in North Africa and Europe during the last one." This was an interesting lesson for me, reduced to just a few words.

Holzer had given me the phone number of an executive with a Ro-Ro service operating out of Southampton to Le Havre. After a brief phone conversation, I arranged to go to the port and watch one of their vessels loading. These vessels were, in essence, very large ferries, with only a single deck, and a stern ramp for the truck-trailer combinations that rolled aboard. There was a simple tariff whereby freight charges were based on the length in linear feet of the total rig, tractor, and trailer. For several hours that evening, I watched the cargo operations. I had been given the use of a small cabin for the overnight trip to Le Havre. It was quite a thrill to cross the English Channel, and I spent several hours on the bridge, by invitation of the Captain, watching the heavy ship traffic in the Channel before going below for a few hours of sleep. Early the next morning, I watched the discharge of trailers and the loading of outbound units. Then I boarded a train to Paris, admiring the lush countryside as we made the run to the French capital.

To say that all this impressed me would be an understatement. I felt like an unintended tourist taking in the sights of London, then Paris. The most lasting memory I have of Paris, aside from the usual attractions, was trying to find a restaurant that first evening and finally ending up in a typical Parisian grill where I was seated against the wall at a long table with four or five locals on each side of me, and a solid row of others facing me. No one offered to speak English, and so I ordered my meal by pointing at something fairly attractive that had been served to one of my table companions. My work in the near future would be limited to the Caribbean and South America, and so years would pass before I became familiar with these two great cities, London and Paris.

Eric Holzer and I often traveled together to the Sun Shipyard in Chester, Pennsylvania, taking the train to Philadelphia and then on by car to Chester and the shipyard. As I boarded the train at Newark, Holzer, who had boarded the train in New York since he lived in the city, would remark to me, "Good morning Art. Are you ready for another interesting visit?" The new Ro-Ro was well along in construction when I first visited the yard. Holzer wanted me to be involved so that I would be fully conversant with the capabilities of the vessel. I participated in all discussions and decisions bearing on trailer and vehicle loading and discharge.

Once loaded on the ship, the trailers would require strong bracing to protect them during transit. There were a number of options, all of which we tested before deciding on a box-like portable support at the front of the trailer, where the connection to the tractor's fifth wheel would be made prior to the trailer's offloading. We were also concerned about the ability of yard tractors to pull loaded trailers up the ramps, particularly the internal, shipboard ramps connecting the various decks. It was a question primarily of the angle of ascent, and I was amazed to learn that a fifteen-degree incline was the steepest possible for a loaded tractor-trailer combination to ascend.

Holzer and I usually spent time at the shipyard with Paul Atkinson, the company president, who wanted to be kept updated on every aspect of the project, but most of our time was spent with the chief naval architect and the construction manager. I would be a weary guy when I finally got home in the evening, but these visits to the shipyard were really stimulating; and this was the only time I was ever directly involved in the design and construction of a seagoing vessel. Since this vessel would be the only Ro-Ro vessel of its kind in the world, nearly everything we did was a first, including the loading and the discharge of some 700 trailers without massive congestion and gridlock. We finally decided to chalk an exact outline of the vessel and ramps on a vacant blacktopped terminal yard in Port Newark, in order to conduct a simulated loading, utilizing a large number of trailers, trucks, and drivers secured from a local trucker. A group of us, including truck-terminal operating specialists, spent several long days on that blacktop until we thought we had it right, even though no one could be fully certain until a loading and a discharge were done live. Nowadays, this rehearsal exercise could easily be done by computer simulation.

With a staff of only four, we were all, by necessity, involved in a variety of tasks essential to the success of our project. One of these tasks was to design a logo for the company to be used on our stationery, displayed on the ship's funnel (smokestack), and on the trailers we would need to augment the fleets of over-the-road trucking equipment provided by trucking companies and used by shippers. Designing a logo was a task I refused to outsource, because I already had a concept in mind, a concept that I worked on again and again at the dining room table at our house in Westfield.

When I finally thought I had it right, I arranged for the finished version to be produced by an outside commercial artist. I was enormously pleased when Messrs. Holzer and Atkinson accepted my design.

Those were stimulating times, perhaps the most interesting of my entire professional career. But just eight months at TTT had passed when I received a call from Grace Line's president, Hal Logan, inviting me to join him for dinner. It was at that dinner that he offered me the opportunity to return to Grace Line, with a commitment to replace him as President. Leaving TTT would be difficult, but a career at Grace Line that would eventually bring me to the top management position had long been my heart's desire, and now it was within reach. I don't recall whether I agreed then or a few days later, but I did accept the offer. I knew Grace extremely well and learned from my continued inside contacts that there were changes taking place that could soon open that door, which, when I had previously left Grace, had not seemed possible, at least not for years to come. Grace Line was an infinitely larger and more complex organization that offered much better compensation. I never had any serious misgivings about leaving TTT, since I was able to move on to much broader horizons than those offered by that company. Still, this was a difficult decision for me to make, and I was somewhat remorseful about leaving. But I reasoned that to become president of Grace Line would fulfill my ultimate ambition, and furthermore it was still early enough in the venture for Eric Holzer to bring in a replacement for me without serious damage to the project.

I advised Holzer by letter on May 5, 1967, which he graciously acknowledged on May 11th. I never saw him become visibly upset about anything, but I'm sure he was disappointed, not resentful, about my leaving. In talks with him, I discussed my opportunity at Grace at length, later expressing my feelings and reasons for my decision in a letter to him. In reply, he wrote, "I had no alternative but to accept your decision in the matter. I made clear to you that I did so with great regret and extreme reluctance. I want to express my appreciation for the very fine work that you did during the short period that you were associated with TTT and thank you for your willingness to remain at our disposal for consultations." One of my concerns at TTT had been Holzer's son, Peter, about thirty years old at the time, and given to meddling in my activities at the company. He was a nice enough person, though a bit arrogant and somewhat spoiled by his father. I hadn't relished the idea of having to work with him or, perhaps, *for* him in the future, and indeed my replacement at TTT did have serious problems with young Peter. Several years after I left the company, Eric Holzer was killed in an automobile accident in

Belgium. Peter replaced him at AUT, which declared bankruptcy a few years later, and TTT was sold to the Puerto Rican government.

*   *   *   *

POSTSCRIPT

Modified versions of the roll-on roll-off vessel introduced to the U.S./Puerto Rican trade in 1967 are still operating in that trade at this writing (2006). An article appearing in the December, 2005, issue of the *AMERICAN SHIPPER* headlines "Sea Star adds ship to Puerto Rico link," going on to say "Sea Star Line L.L.C. that provides services between the U.S. mainland and Puerto Rico said it will add a third ship to its fleet," adding, "The *El Faro* is a sister ship of the *El Yunque* and the *El Morro,* deployed in the Jacksonville/San Juan trade in 1998 and 1999, respectively. The three vessels are each 30 years old." The major difference between these vessels and the original TTT vessel is that they have been modified from pure roll-on/roll-off vessels to Ro-Ro-container configurations, taking a full load of stacked containers on the main deck.

Chapter 5

GRACE LINE ROUND TWO

I was induced to return to Grace Line in May, 1967, by Hal Logan, who by then was the last man standing of the leading contenders, Mike Diaz, Andrew Gibson, and himself, to replace Wilfred J. McNeil as president. Logan's first step in that direction had been announced in the *New York Times* on May 22, 1964, in an article reporting that he had been named senior vice president at Grace Line, "responsible in the field of corporate administration, coordinating the overall activities of the company." Logan's new position effectively elevated him over Diaz and Gibson, who were extremely upset by the move and soon resigned; and in early 1967 he replaced McNeil as president. Logan's commitment to me was that he would groom me as his successor, hoping to move on to a senior executive position in Grace Line's parent company, W. R. Grace, a much larger and more diversified organization, where there would be greater opportunities for advancement. My return to Grace Line was announced in a May 18, 1967, press release and appeared in the *Journal of Commerce* several days later.

I was named senior vice president, with responsibility for the sales activities of all Grace Line's Atlantic Coast services, as well as the line's operations between Atlantic ports in the United States and the Caribbean and the North Coast of South America. My new position became effective on May 18, 1967, just short of ten years after my employment by Grace Line in July 1957. Jim Hoyt, one of the trainees recruited from the Ivy League before then, was also promoted. That left the Ivy League group of Hoyt, Ernest Senn, Edward Meyer, and Albert Wenzell; Donald Grimm, a former assistant to Logan in the Department of Defense; and me as the senior management of the company. Grimm was the company's chief financial officer; Senn headed U.S. Pacific Coast operations and was based in San Francisco with Wenzell as his deputy; and Meyer was in charge of the Passenger Division.

The eighteen months that followed were a busy time for me. Not only did I head the sales department, I was charged with directing a major profit center. Even so, this was truly the essential crash course for a plausible candidate aiming to become the company's next president. A document prepared by Hal Logan for the parent company shortly after I returned, "Appraisal of Functions: Grace Line Inc.," stated:

Caribbean Service: Here we have "newcomers" assigned in an attempt to bring innovation and black ink to a sick service. So far we have had good performance based in a break with tradition, i.e. going to contract stevedoring, moving to Pier 40, study of new ships of revolutionary types, and closer working arrangements with the National Flag Carrier – CAVN. We will continue to develop this management by exposure to more traditional methods in Grace Line and other steamship companies and attendance at seminars involving other industries.

Key members of my staff and I were the "newcomers," and Logan's reference to closer working arrangements with CAVN, the Venezuelan Line, the national-flag carrier of Venezuela, was a consequence of the challenges posed by rising nationalism in Venezuela and other countries served by Grace Line, which threatened Grace Line's domination of its traditional trade lanes. The challenge lay in government-owned or government-supported steamship lines: in Venezuela, the government owned Venezuelan Line (CAVN); in Colombia, the Flota Mercante Grandcolombiana Line, owned by the Colombian Coffee Federation, comprised of the major coffee grower-exporters; and, in Chile, the *Chilean Line,* privately owned but operating with the full backing and support of the Chilean government. While these national-flag services were generally inferior to those of Grace Line in terms of the age, size, and speed of their vessels; the frequency of their sailings, and the quality of their customer service, they had one significant advantage: each of these countries not only had regulations in place requiring import licenses for all incoming shipments, but further required that at least 50 percent of such licenses bear a stamp requiring shipment by the country's national-flag line. This requirement was a clear case of discrimination against American-flag carriers and conflicted with U.S. shipping laws that contained protections against such unduly discriminatory practices.

Grace Line, with the support of the Federal Maritime Commission (FMC), whose mission included the protection of American-flag shipping from discrimination by foreign governments, attempted to negotiate agreements with the three lines involved which would provide for modifications in their routing requirements so that American-flag carriers were given the same status as the national-flag carriers of the three countries. When these negotiations failed, countervailing rules were enacted by the Commission, requiring a minimum of 50 percent of U.S. exports to Venezuela to move on American-Flag ships, with the implied threat that similar actions against Colombia and Chile could follow. The enactment of these rules forced the national-flag lines to the bargaining table, and agreements requiring reciprocal treatment were concluded and filed with the FMC. The formula finally embodied in these cargo-sharing agreements gave national shipping lines, U.S. and foreign, equal rights to participate in the volume of traffic generated by their trade, with third parties carrying the residual. For example, under a 40:40:20 cargo-sharing agreement, each of the bilateral traders reserved 40 percent of the cargo for its national vessels and cross-traders carried the remaining 20 percent of the cargo. (Source: *MARITIME ECONOMIC* by Martin Stopford.)

One of my new responsibilities was to build and maintain good relations with the chief executives of the Venezuelan Line and Flota Mercante Grancolombiana, and, eventually, with the chief executive of the Chilean Line. There seemed to be an unending stream of disagreements between us, largely because the reciprocal routing agreements were difficult to administer so as to ensure an equitable distribution of cargoes. Both sides constantly strove to improve market share, but with Grace Line having the better service and the significant benefit of cargoes moving to subsidiaries of W.R. Grace, it was difficult for the counterpart national-flag lines to obtain the equal share of the routed imports to which they were entitled under the agreements.

I frequently met with Dr. Marquez-Añez, president of the Venezuelan Line, in attempts to resolve such issues, hosting meetings in New York. Marquez-Añez, who spoke little English, had a doctorate in economics and was a tough negotiator, seemingly never fully satisfied with the outcome of our meetings. He was short in stature, with intense black eyes that seemed to spark when he made his strident demands. Our discussions with him were a far cry from the amiable meetings with our customers to which I was accustomed. With a poor grasp of the Spanish language, I depended on George Spiotta, then our vice president of operations for the Caribbean, who spoke excellent Spanish, to serve as our interpreter. George was a close friend and a fellow Kings Pointer. He had spent years working for the Grace organization in South America and in addition to his excellent interpersonal skills, he instinctively understood and responded to the Latin business culture. He maintained close relationships with his counterparts in the Venezuelan Line, and was indispensable in making our relationship with the Venezuelan Line a viable one.

Occasionally we met with Dr. Marquez-Añez on board the Santa Rosa or Santa Paula, while they were in New York. My thought was that these luxury cargo/passenger vessels reflected the eminent position occupied by Grace Line in the Venezuelan trade, and should impress upon the good doctor what a powerful ally we could be in developing our mutual interests. While W. R. Grace had no subsidiary companies in Venezuela, Grace Line interests were well looked after by our agents of many years, Boulton & Cia. With a hundred-year history of business in Venezuela extending back to the first Boulton, an English sea captain who decided to tie his future to the developing country, the company had become a leading firm in Venezuela and the major ship agent, stevedore, and terminal operator in the country.

Boulton was the principal owner of Avensa, a major airline that connected Caracas with the United States and other countries, and the principal owner of other local industries. W. R. Grace also had airline interests, as part owner of Panagra Airlines, in partnership with Pan American Airways. Panagra provided service from New York and Miami to the major cities of Colombia, Ecuador, Peru, Bolivia, and Chile. This was an impressive business credential in our dealings with our new partners in Latin America.

Meetings with Marquez-Añez, while contentious, were usually productive. I clearly recall our first meeting on the Santa Rosa. Having arrived at her berth at Pier 40 only a few hours earlier, the ship was still in the throes of disembarking her passengers and commencing cargo operations. With a frenzy of activity around us, George Spiotta and I boarded with Marquez-Añez and his deputy in tow. We made our way into the spacious atrium and settled into soft leather couches, waiting for the main dining room to be cleared and a table to be set up for our lunch. Our guest looked small and unthreatening as he sank back into the cushions, his dark eyes darting back and forth visibly impressed with the tempo of activity. "So, Novacek, you and George bring me here because you think that this fancy ship will make me more agreeable," he said in his deep voice, so unexpected from a man of his stature. Then the bargaining began, lasting through our lunch and well into the afternoon. I enjoyed these business skirmishes, and George and I would later engage in lengthy post mortems of the events, hoping to ensure that we really understood what had been agreed upon.

Collaboration with the Venezuelan Line eventually led to another first in the maritime industry, a vessel-sharing agreement filed with the FMC, a practice quite common in shipping today. But at that time, such cooperative agreements to share carrier space did not exist. Each carrier was its own brand, represented by its vessels and their stack markings. Conventional wisdom said that the esteemed Grace Line would never let itself carry shipments under a Venezuelan Line bill of lading, and the old hands there were horrified at the idea. On top of that, many shippers were confused too, but we went ahead and did it anyway. One week a Grace Line freighter would load all cargoes for both carriers, and the next week it would be a Venezuelan Line freighter loading the cargoes, both using Grace Line's pier 40 on the North River at an enormous savings in vessel operating expense. We were now successfully producing the "black ink" Hal Logan had called for in his "Appraisal" of Grace Line's Caribbean services.

The sharing agreement did not apply to the *Santa Rosa* and *Santa Paula,* which were themselves marketing tools, since many important Venezuelan businessmen used these vessels as their preferred choice of transportation to and from the United States. However, being a "vessel-sharing" partner with Grace Line on freighter service brought shipper acceptance of Venezuelan Line's services that until then had been forced by import license requirements, which many shippers found distasteful. In those days, when passenger ships were the principal mode of ocean travel, there was an axiom: "the cargo follows the passengers." With the development of reliable, scheduled airline service, there is no longer a demand for passenger-ship travel. Today's passenger ships, "cruise ships" in actuality, are huge floating resorts that do not pretend to offer passage to a particular destination and do not carry cargo.

As the two national-flag carriers, Grace Line and Venezuelan Line met with little competition from other lines, generally referred to as third-flag or cross-carriers. There was a strong steamship conference in place in the U.S.-Venezuela trade, with the conference offices within walking distance of the Grace Line offices. Conference meetings were held on an as-needed basis, and I frequently attended. This was certainly a far cry from my days at the independent, firmly anti-conference Isbrandtsen Steamship Line. The conference member lines were bound by the tariff filed with the Federal Maritime Commission, and the meetings usually dealt with rate requests made by shippers. The tariff was based on a dual-rate system whereby signatories were offered the lower of two rates. The dual-rate system, permitted by U.S. maritime law, was a formidable weapon in ensuring that shippers did not use non-conference lines, and the cargo and vessel sharing agreements, in turn, made it difficult for third-flag carriers, who were conference members, to survive in these trades. With these safeguards protecting Grace Line and its national-flag counterparts from serious competition, rate levels in the trades serviced by Grace Line were among the highest in the world.

Another factor was also in play. The successful opposition of port labor groups to the introduction of containerships into the Venezuelan trade experienced by Grace Line in 1960 was duplicated among port labor groups in all major South American ports and would take years to overcome. Consequently, Grace Line did not have to face the competition of this innovative manner of handling cargoes, the use of containers, a practice already revolutionizing the U.S.-European and U.S.-Far East trades. At the time, cargo-handling expenses represented at least 50 percent of all costs. Fully containerized ships were able to reduce that cost to around 15 to 20 percent. Equally important was the fact that while a traditional cargo ship spent about 40 percent of its time in port, in-port time for a comparable containership was only about 17 percent, as a consequence of the development of container terminals with huge gantry cranes that could handle as many as thirty lifts (the discharge and loading of containers) per hour. (Source: *MARITIME ECONOMICS* by Martin Stopford).

Having disposed of its two fully containerized ships after the debacle in Venezuela, it was not necessary for Grace to undertake the capital investment required in building new containerships or by converting existing tonnage, as Atlantic carriers were being forced to do as a consequence of Sea-Land's entry into the U.S.-European trade lanes in 1966. The so-called container revolution was a dramatic development in maritime trade, credited to a trucker, Malcom P. McLean, who later recalled that in 1937 he had driven a load of cotton bales from Fayetteville, NC, to Hoboken, NJ and, in his own words:

> *I had to wait most of the day to deliver the bales, sitting in my truck, watching the stevedores load other cargo It struck me that I was looking at a lot of wasted time and money. I watched them take each crate out of a truck, slip it into a sling, then lift it into the hold of a ship. Once in the hold, every sling had to be unloaded, and the cargo stowed where it was to go. As I waited around that day, I had the thought that it would be easier to lift my trailer up, without any of the contents being touched, and put it on the ship.*
>
> (Source: *AMERICAN SHIPPER,* July 2001)

That casual observation by a 24-year old would, in time, change the ways of commerce worldwide. By 1950, McLean Industries had become one of the most successful transport businesses in the United States. In 1955, the company acquired a small tanker company, Pan Atlantic, and adapted two of the decks on one its T-2 tankers, the *Ideal-X,* by adding a platform for trailers. On April 26, 1956, the *Ideal-X* sailed between Port Newark, NJ, and Houston, carrying on its deck 58 reinforced truck trailers, each measuring 33 by 8 feet. Two years later, the first "pure" containership, McLean's *Gateway City,* started regular service between New York, Florida, and Texas. In 1958, Pan Atlantic introduced containership service to Puerto Rico with the sailing of the *SS Fairland,* and, in 1960, the company changed its name to Sea-Land. (Source: *History of Sea-land Timeline,* Sea-Land Alumni.com)

Grace Line executives followed the remarkable success of Sea-Land with considerable unease. I recall attending a meeting chaired by Grace Line's then President, Wilfred McNeil, who was asked about the potential competition of Sea-Land (already successfully established in the Puerto Rican trade) to Grace Line's Caribbean island services to Curacao, Aruba, Jamaica, Santo Domingo, and Haiti. "The Caribbean is and will remain a Grace Line lake," he firmly replied, adding, "Sea-Land may be doing well in the domestic trades, but going into our trade lanes is another matter altogether. The Puerto Rican trade, protected by U.S. law against foreign competition, is one thing, but going up against a subsidized carrier in international trade is quite another matter." In those days, I tended to believe and accept his opinions. After all, he was a former deputy secretary of defense. Now I realize that there is no substitute for getting down into the trenches and organizing your counter-offensive.

I had been exposed to Sea-Land's service several years earlier when, as Grace Line's traffic manager for the Caribbean, I had assisted Hal Logan in an abortive attempt to enter the Puerto Rican trade (considered a domestic trade), and thus find a further source of cargo for the two container vessels we had scheduled to serve Venezuelan ports. This was to be accomplished by calling at San Juan en route to La Guaira. My task at the time was to develop a tariff and a marketing plan in conjunction with the firm Grace Line had selected as their agents in Puerto Rico. I arrived in San Juan, my first time there, joining Andy Gibson, who was there to make arrangements for our use of a container terminal. Grace Line was in a regulatory action before the Federal Maritime Commission, seeking commission approval to begin this service in a trade where American-flag tonnage was mandatory, a requirement met by our two container vessels. The issue was that Grace Line's services were subsidized, and subsidized vessels were not permitted in the domestic trades. The essence of the Grace proposal was to carve out that portion of the operating subsidy represented by the time required for the diversion to San Juan and exclude it from subsidy payments. Gibson took me under his wing as we toured the terminal assigned to Sea-Land at the Puerto Nuevo complex in San Juan port. There we viewed row after row of Sea-Land trailers (containers on chassis), assembled in a vast, asphalt-surfaced container yard, in the shadow of the imposing gantry cranes provided by

Sea-Land, an early version of the carrier-controlled yards that Sea-Land would eventually have around the globe.

I was successful in my limited mission, developing a tariff to be filed with the Interstate Commerce Commission and formulating a marketing plan, but Grace Line was never able to get the U.S. government approval it needed. Sea-Land by then was established in the Puerto Rican trade, with the first deep-sea pure containership service in any U.S. trade route, and strenuously opposed our entry there. The traditional carrier of many years standing, the highly respected Bull Line, had already been forced to close down its breakbulk service to Puerto Rico in the face of the container revolution that Sea-Land had introduced in its first conquest in the Caribbean.

It was on this, my initial visit to Puerto Rico that I was first exposed to the system that Sea-Land would use to "feeder" lower-volume ports by the employment of small foreign-flagged container ships. Containers destined from U.S. mainland ports to Caribbean ports other than San Juan, all of which were serviced by Grace Line at the time, were transferred to and from Sea-Land chartered feeders and mainline ships at the San Juan terminal. This was the beginning of the end for the century-old Grace Line services in the Caribbean, despite Wilfred McNeil's denials. But I would encounter Sea-Land again during my TTT days, and later, when I went head-to-head with Sea-Land as an executive at Seatrain Line.

Unbelievably, for a while it was business as usual at Grace Line, still only marginally affected by the advent of containerization. The company operated six cargo passenger ships and eighteen freighters, providing American-flag service on four major trade routes between the United States and the Caribbean and Central and South America. But, prompted by the dynamics of the post-World War II maritime industry, the stage had been set for other changes that would significantly impact my career. How these dynamics affected Grace Line through the growth of national-flag lines and the early stages of the container revolution has already been touched upon. The decision of W.R. Grace to concentrate on the expansion of its growing industrial specialty chemicals and consumer products operations in the United States would have an even more profound effect. But all this still lay in the future on the day I was informed of my appointment as president of Grace Line.

I remember that day in October of 1968 well. The appointment certainly didn't come as a surprise, so I will never really understand why I promptly suffered one of the biggest moments of self-doubt in my life. Seldom lacking in confidence before, I suddenly realized that I was expected to run this major shipping company and I didn't quite know where to begin. As I left Hal Logan's office, I stepped into the elevator and was so dazed that I failed to get off at my floor and found myself in the lobby. Strangely, my lips began to swell and, because then I could not face anyone in the company, I left the building and began walking the streets of downtown New York. I must have walked for nearly two hours before my lips returned to their normal size.

The New President of Grace Line, October 1968

I finally realized that, nearing age forty, I was probably as ready as I would ever be for this major responsibility, even though I had no significant background in marine vessel or terminal operations, and no background at all in the passenger side of the business. But I was a professional in the commercial side of liner shipping, which to my mind drives the operating groups, and I simply would have to apply myself to better understand the workings of the passenger department. Back to the office I went, immediately calling a meeting of all the managers and briefing them on my intention to keep the company on course. I then met with each manager individually, repeating my assurances, to make certain that everyone knew it was to be business as usual.

My time as president was one of anticipation, but it ended in disappointment. Grace Line was replacing its older vessels with much larger ships, built explicitly for their specific trades and incorporating many innovative features that resulted from in-depth studies of the principal commodities moving in each trade lane. Somehow, Grace Line seemed oblivious to the success of fully-containerized vessels in other U.S. trades, and we were damn-well going to build our own specialized vessels. The most remarkable of these purpose-built ships were the four M-Class vessels, the *Santas Magdalena*, *Mercedes*, *Maria*, and *Monica*, designed to serve the trade between New York and the West Coast of South America, calling at Panama, transiting the Panama Canal, and then on to the ports of Buenaventura, Colombia; Guayaquil, Ecuador; and Callao, Peru; then returning over the same route.

The M-Class vessels, with gantry cranes that ran fore and aft on rails running the length of the main deck, were capable of self-loading and discharging several hundred 20-foot

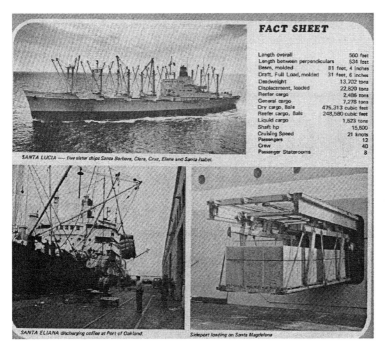

SANTA LUCIA — five sister ships Santa Barbara, Clara, Cruz, Elena and Santa Isabel.

SANTA ELIANA discharging coffee at Port of Oakland.   Sideport loading on Santa Magdalena.

FACT SHEET

Length overall	560 feet
Length between perpendiculars	534 feet
Beam, molded	81 feet, 4 inches
Draft, Full Load, molded	31 feet, 6 inches
Deadweight	13,702 tons
Displacement, loaded	22,820 tons
Reefer cargo	2,486 tons
General cargo	7,276 tons
Dry cargo, Bale	475,313 cubic feet
Reefer cargo, Bale	248,580 cubic feet
Liquid cargo	1,623 tons
Shaft hp	15,500
Cruising Speed	21 knots
Passengers	12
Crew	40
Passenger Staterooms	8

containers. These units were specially designed to transport a "chop" of coffee (250 bags) northbound from Buenaventura. Each had original fabricated interior wall linings that would permit the capture and disposal of moisture resulting from the humidity created by the bagged coffee. These same containers were used on the southbound voyage for the handling of general cargo. The M-ships were also fitted with side ports, large doors in the sides of the vessel that allowed bananas to be loaded in Ecuador and discharged in

New York through the use of conveyer belts. Thus configured, these ships could handle all types of packaged cargoes. Since the 'tween-deck space exceeded the container capacity, port labor in Peru, Ecuador, and Columbia did not object to working containers. It also helped to have the local political muscle offered by the Grace y Cia Companies in these West Coast South American countries. Further, the M-Class vessels had first-class facilities accommodating 125 passengers. Passenger ships were given priority berthing in South American ports, where congestion causing vessel-docking delays was a common occurrence, and this was another plus for our ships.

There was also a fleet of sister freighters, known as the *Lucia* Class, designed to use traditional cargo-handling methods to load and discharge almost any type of cargo, including heavy lifts of up to 75 tons, and some 20-foot containers on deck. While the line of *Santa Lucia* class freighters could be used in any breakbulk general cargo trade, the same was not true of the M-Class, designed, as they were, for the carriage of bananas and coffee northbound from Ecuador and Colombia. On the other hand, fully containerized ships, such as those developed by Sea-Land, could not readily be moved from one trade lane to another unless they were provided functional terminals that included shore-side gantry cranes and container handling equipment, accommodations that today are found in every major port in the world.

Totally concentrating on my new responsibilities as president, I was not fully conscious of the quiet efforts of Hal Logan, our chairman, and J. Peter Grace, president of W.R. Grace & Co., to sell Grace Line, nor what such a sale could mean to me. I had been assured that in the event of a change of ownership, our management team would continue in place, since, after all, we were running a going, profitable company. How naive! But then, I was young, and had no experience in how takeovers so often work, but sell us they did. Grace Line was sold to Prudential Line, Hal Logan moved to a senior position at W.R. Grace, and I was left to the mercies of the new owners, Spyros Skouras and his son, who bore the same name.

When two companies are merged, something has to give. Even though Grace Line was by far the larger and in my opinion the better-managed of the two, after the sale, Prudential Line employees were given job preference. The next few months were pure hell as one after another of Grace Line's long-time employees was let go. I was present when Jim Hoyt was called to the younger Skouras's office and told, "Jim, we're building a young team of managers here, and you don't fit into our future plans." Jim was 50, and I figured that at 39 I was safe. My brain was picked in a series of management meetings where I briefed the new owners about all the Grace Line services, particularly the capabilities and trade lanes of the new vessels. I still had the title of president, and I reported to Spyros the younger. He was about five years older than I, slender and shorter, with reddish hair. My old mentor, Mike Diaz, had once said that the young Skouras, with his long neck, a crop of slicked-back hair, and a receding chin, looked like a plucked rooster.

The elder Skouras was a truly remarkable person. In his mid-80's, he was quite the opposite of his son. Short and heavy-set, he walked with a cane. He was born and grew up in Greece, immigrating to the United States and ultimately becoming Chairman of 20th Century Fox Film Corporation, one of the world's major film producers and owner of a network of movie theaters. I can see him now, sitting in a straight-backed chair, leaning forward, slumped on his cane, an observer at one of our management meetings. His eyes would close as though he were asleep. But then, when some difficult or unresolved matter arose, he would suddenly open his eyes and ask a question that invariably would go to the crux of the matter, making it possible for us to make a decision and move on.

Prudential Line had a shipbuilding program of its own, involving the construction of four LASH (lighter aboard ship) vessels. These ships were huge, designed to carry lighters (barges) with dimensions that would permit their use in European canals and rivers. The concept was to load the barges with various kinds of cargo at the origin point; for example, river ports on the Mississippi, float them aboard the LASH vessel, and then float them off at the destination ports of call, moving them to their final destinations via inland waterways. I'll never forget visiting the Avondale Shipyard in Mississippi in company with young Spyros and Andrew Gibson, the Maritime Administrator, a former

Grace Line executive and a good friend, for the keel-laying ceremony of the first such vessel. Gibson was there because the government was providing a differential subsidy for the construction of the ship, the subsidy, as noted earlier, representing compensation for the difference in shipbuilding costs in U.S. shipyards and those in less costly foreign shipyards, and a ship mortgage guarantee of Prudential-Grace Line's construction loans.

Art, Andrew Gibson (Federal Maritime Administrator), and Spyros Skouras (far right) Avondale Shipyard, 1970

I was asked by young Spyros, "Well Art, what do think of her?" I paused for a moment, and replied, "Too bad this beauty isn't designed to carry cargo containers instead of barges, because that's where the future lies." This was not what he wanted to hear, and my remark did not improve our relationship.

One day shortly after my visit to the shipyard, I received a call from the elder Skouras's secretary informing me that the two of them would like me to join them for lunch at India House, directly across the street on Hanover Square. I thought that perhaps they were going to clarify my position with the company, but it did not occur to me that such clarification might not be to my liking. Shortly after we sat down and placed our luncheon orders, it happened. The old man looked at me, trying to be congenial, and said "Art, we have a problem. It's nothing to do with the caliber of your work, but we simply can't have two presidents; and since Spyros is my son, I have to give him the position." I was shocked, but I should have seen it coming. "Furthermore," he continued, "I think that it is best that you leave the company, since to stay is not good for you or my son."

I have largely managed to erase from my memory the few weeks I remained at the company, wrapping up some loose ends. I had never been fired before, and I couldn't accept the idea. But I started scrambling for another job.

Long after I left Prudential-Grace Line and the construction of the LASH ships was completed, they were placed in the trade lanes between the U.S. and Europe, but most shippers preferred to use cargo containers carried on fast containerships, door-to-door. LASH ships were eventually relegated to handling foreign aid and military cargoes, with some even being converted to containerships. A few years later, Prudential-Grace Line declared bankruptcy and was forced to sell the Grace Line portion of the company to Delta Line. And who became president of the newly purchased line? My old friend, Andy Gibson.

*   *   *   *

POSTSCRIPT

Prudential's Sale Of South American Operations

Board Chairman Skouras Condemns "Disastrous Business Environment" In Mediterranean

Prudential Lines has announced that it plans to sell its South American shipping operations to Delta Steamship Lines. The $75-million sale, which still requires review and approval by U.S. regulatory authorities, comprises Prudential's Atlantic and Pacific divisions with 12 ships (six L-class, two Jet-class, four combination cargo/passenger M-class vessels) and the take-over by Delta of two chartered cargoliners. Prudential will continue to operate its Mediterranean division which is served by the company's LASH vessels.

In this exclusive interview with editor Marc Felice, Prudential Lines chairman and chief executive officer Spyros S. Skouras speaks about the reasons that led to his decision to divest himself of a profitable operation and the major part of his company's fleet. He then discusses the impact this will have on the company, and his plans for the future.

Skouras

Felice: *What caused you to decide to sell the major part of Prudential's fleet to Delta Line?*

Skouras: It was my appraisal of the future in the shipping industry regardless where, or what routes or what services are being offered. Because of the increased costs due to the inflationary spiral, there is now a strong requirement for a consolidation of companies to meet the foreign competition. Therefore, the question before me was: Shall I buy or shall I sell? — The company was not in a position to buy. So, there was no choice for me but to sell.

Felice: *I believe that the ships and the two routes you sold were profitable. You sold them in spite of their profitability?*

Skouras: Yes, they were profitable. But the idea is to keep them profitable for the future. That's why I believe the consolidation of companies is necessary, to save on many expenses which are accrued to a larger operation.

Felice: *Conversely, I believe that the Mediterranean operation, which will continue as Prudential's, has not been profitable?*

Skouras: We have not been profitable in the Mediterranean for the last two years. But this does not necessarily mean that we will not be profitable in the future.

Abandoning Old Itinerary

About one year ago, in July of 1976, to be exact, we were forced to depart from our routine itinerary which we had followed for the last 17 years. We had to abandon our service to Spain, Italy and Greece because of the tremendous overtonnaging on this route, which in turn led to tremendous malpractices. These malpractices were of such a nature that we found it impossible to secure enough cargo for our ships to make it sufficiently attractive to stay in this operation. We had to give up between 30 to 40 million dollars of business in an area that we had served for 17 years. It was not an easy decision for us to make.

Within a few months after we departed from that trade route, Atlantica Line, a containership operator with 32 percent of the Italian westbound business and a large percentage of the Spanish business also abandoned this service.

Many people thought that it was the question of the right hardware. But it had nothing to do with that. Whether containers or barges — both companies had concluded that to remain in such a disastrous business environment would but lead to further losses.

So, we at Prudential changed our Mediterranean itinerary and we serve now Morocco, Algeria, Libya, Egypt, Syria, Turkey, Rumania and Russia. And I am very happy to state that our decision to make the change appears to have been correct. Although it was an expensive change for the first year, it has been a successful transition and we look forward to increase our business in that area as the countries we now serve are developing and their trade expands.

Forced Out

Felice: *You mentioned "a disastrous business environment." Do you mean to say that Prudential was forced out of the Mediterranean business because of unscrupulous operations by some competitors?*

Skouras: No question! that's exactly what I was trying to point out.

Chapter 6

SEATRAIN LINE

It was June, 1970, and my last few weeks at Grace Line were devoted to finding another job. It's unnerving to have a wife, five kids, a mortgage, and no paycheck coming in. It wasn't that I wasn't trying, for even prior to my fateful lunch with Spyros Skouras and his son I had begun looking around at the job market. I had been approached by an executive-search firm on behalf of Maersk Line (today the largest containership line in the world) regarding a position as general manager in the United States for their planned containership services. I flew to Copenhagen on a Friday overnight flight, arriving Saturday morning, checked into a hotel, and, after a couple of hours' sleep, walked across the square to the Maersk headquarters building for my interview. The red-brick building occupied half a block and was surrounded by similar buildings, all in the late-19th century, plain utilitarian style, well suited to a company that traced its maritime history back more than a hundred years. Maersk was the largest commercial enterprise in Denmark, with a huge fleet of cargo ships, tankers, and specialized vessels; shipyards; and related industries.

I was ushered into a spacious room furnished with an antique conference table and chairs, its walls bearing portraits of a succession of the company's owners and pictures of Maersk Line vessels. Three senior company executives sat at one end of the conference table and I sat at the other. "Well, Novacek, we see you've made it all right -- hope you are not too tired from your flight." Even though I could barely keep my eyes open, I responded as brightly as I could, "I feel fine and I'm looking forward to our conversation." What followed was a three-hour grilling, briefly interrupted by a quick sandwich lunch at the table. Apparently, it was company practice for management to come in on Saturdays for a half-day, and they had scheduled my meeting with them accordingly.

I must have done well enough at that interview to make the shortlist of prospects, for I received a call at my hotel room that afternoon inviting me to join the firm's owner, Maersk Moller, and his wife for dinner at Tivoli Gardens, Copenhagen's exquisite outdoor entertainment center. It's a fenced-in area about a half-mile long and four blocks wide, embracing lakes, walkways with benches, restaurants, a Ferris wheel and other rides, taverns, games of chance, marching bands, and an outdoor concert area with wooden folding chairs and a stage.

We met at the Tivoli's entrance, by the turnstiles, introduced ourselves, and leisurely strolled about, enjoying the park's attractions, talking mostly about my impressions of Copenhagen. Moller was a tall, slender man, handsome and dignified, about 50, and his wife was his graceful and demure counterpart. Our destination was one of Tivoli's excellent restaurants, and they were delightful hosts, putting me quickly at ease. I don't recall the details of our conversation, which dealt with my personal background and work experience. There was some mention of Hans Isbrandtsen, my first employer and Maersk Moller's cousin. (The two had had a falling-out during the war years when they were together in New York, representing the Danish maritime shipping industry.) All in all, it was an immensely enjoyable evening.

Shortly after returning to the States, I received a call from the search firm, advising me that I was one of the leading candidates for the job, but that Maersk was not yet ready to launch its container services, and thus no decision would be made for several months. But I couldn't wait that long to find out whether I would be the chosen one. Some six months later, when I was already employed by Seatrain, a ranking executive from the U.S. trucking industry was selected for the Maersk position. He was a second-generation Danish-American, which may have influenced the decision. At this writing (2006), Mr. Moller is still alive, in his 90's, and still presiding over his global maritime business empire.

Earlier that year, at an industry luncheon, I sat at the same table as Howard Pack, one of the two owners of Seatrain, the other being Joe Kahn. I had heard many interesting things about their company which was then in the midst of a major service expansion into the U.S.-Europe trade, and had a fleet of large containerships under construction. I introduced myself to Pack, and in return received a limp handshake and a few perfunctory comments. Sitting in my office during my last days at Grace Line, I remembered that luncheon and called Pack, expressing my interest in joining his company. Our conversation was brief, with Pack quickly responding, "You'll have to talk to Bill Cole, the executive VP of our container division. He's at the offices in Edgewater. He handles such matters." (Pack's reference was to Edgewater, NJ.)

I called Cole, and several days later we had lunch at one of New York's fancier uptown restaurants, the Four Seasons. He was about 5-9 in height, built like a college wrestler, and, according to him, had served in Navy underwater demolition, the forerunner of the Navy Seals. He had a large head, thinning brown hair, a rugged, expressive face, and pale blue eyes. His ancestry was Welsh, and he looked like one of the coal miners in the 1941 movie "How Green Was My Valley." After some discussion, he said to me, "Art, you're the kind of young executive we're looking for to build our management team." Cole thought the productivity cut-off age for managers was 40, his age. I was 43, a bit old by his standard, but I had far more experience in liner shipping than he. (His previous service had been in ship chartering, where he was considered a star performer.) He offered me the title of senior vice president, with responsibility for Seatrain's Caribbean and South American services. His offer was confirmed by letter a few days later, on March 17, 1970. I accepted the job, agreeing to start in 10 days, which allowed me time for a short vacation and some respite from recent tumultuous events.

I promptly called the Nadals, Grace Line's agents in Haiti, and took them up on their invitation to spend some vacation time with them. Jeanette and I arrived in the bustling, dilapidated airport in Port-au-Prince, and were whisked by limousine to the Nadal estate in the nearby village of Petainville. We were escorted to a lovely guesthouse behind the home of Jean Claude Nadal. After enjoying a day or so of relaxation and the gracious hospitality of our hosts, we moved on to a resort called Ibo Beach, which was under construction by the owner of the Ibolaili Hotel, one of the finest in Haiti. Ibo Beach was on a small island accessed by a 50-mile drive from Port-au-Prince followed by a 30-minute cruise in a motor launch. By no means a luxury facility, Ibo Beach consisted mostly of a series of concrete-block units with thatched roofs and basic plumbing, just steps from a small beach. There was also a sprawling restaurant and bar area with a dozen tables under thatched umbrellas, where, weather permitting, guests could gather for cocktails or outdoor dining.

I am elaborating on this period of my life because at the time I was suffering from what I now realize was severe depression. I was in a highly anxious state and had great difficulty sleeping. Worse yet, I thought I would probably be unable to cope with the future. As it happened, the owner of the beach resort and the Ibolaili Hotel was also a doctor of medicine, spending time at Ibo Beach to supervise the construction and expansion of the small resort. I decided to bring my problems to him, and, with considerable understatement, said, "I'm having trouble sleeping. Is there something you can prescribe?" In reply, he asked, "Do you have any idea what may be causing it?" Reputedly a fine doctor, he proved to be a kindly man, and soon I was relating to him the recent unnerving events of my life. With his wise counseling (we talked every day) supported by a few sleeping pills, I began to feel better, my mood and my sleep steadily improving.

Meanwhile, the freight sales manager for Nadal had invited me on a duck-hunting trip. It was about 5:30 a.m. when the motorboat dropped me ashore where he and three friends were waiting. "Here, this is an extra shotgun for you. You do know how to use it?" "Sure," I lied, never having fired a shotgun in my life. The ensuing events proved how little prepared I was. We motored to a region of swamplands and rice paddies, where a dozen tall, slender locals, dressed in loincloths, met us to serve as our beaters. They circled far ahead of us and disappeared into the swamplands, behind patches of brush and small trees; and when positioned, banged old pots and pans together to roust the ducks for our shooting pleasure. We were spread out at fifty-foot intervals, waist-deep in the water, with our guns raised above our heads. Suddenly, the sky overhead was blanketed by a vast covey of ducks, herons, and a few cranes, quacking and squawking. Gunshots burst around me, and ducks were falling from the sky into the brackish water. When I decided I'd better shoot, I did, and then watched with dismay as a brilliant white crane fell from the sky, having had the misfortune of flying into the shot from the battered weapon I fired.

Although I could see their amused looks, my hunting companions made no mention of my marksmanship as the beaters gathered the fallen ducks. On the way back to our vehicles, dripping with mud, we stopped at a creek brimming with water from a recent rain, stripped off our clothes and waded in, much to the amusement of the locals standing along the banks, men and women alike. At the end of the hunt, even though I was certainly not entitled to them, I was generously given two of the ducks which I took back to be cooked at the resort, sharing them with Jeannette and the doctor. Both ducks had been banded by someone in the United States, probably for some sort of study of wildfowl migration, before they made their doomed flight south for the winter.

*   *   *   *

Back in the U.S., and after a 45-minute drive from my home in Westfield to Edgewater, NJ, I was astonished to see that Seatrain's container division headquarters were housed in several large Quonset-style structures. I learned, however, that a headquarters building was under construction in Weehawken that would face a new finger-pier container terminal jutting into the Hudson River. The terminal had two gantry cranes capable of lifting containers on and off the largest container vessels in service at the time, which included the ships Seatrain had under construction. The nuclear staff at the Container Division was immersed in plans and programs for the new ships and services.

Messrs. Howard Pack and Joe Khan had been in the fur trade after World War II and had only recently become maritime-industry entrepreneurs. Thus they were innovative and unrestrained by the industry's traditional practices and procedures. Howard Pack, brilliant enough to serve on the team that cracked the Japanese secret codes during World War II, was the creative force behind the company's planning that so often confounded competitors. Joe Kahn was a soft-spoken, persuasive man who brought Pack's ideas to fruition with a velvet touch. While Howard could be exasperating at times, one couldn't help liking Joe. The two men had achieved considerable financial success by restructuring wartime-built vessels to make them capable of handling a wide range of cargoes for the military, as well as converting old T2 tankers for carrying bulk grain cargoes shipped under various U.S. aid programs. A division of Seatrain was also heavily involved in the charter market, matching full loads of cargo with vessels under charter.

Pack and Kahn, as they were known, had purchased Seatrain Line several years before I joined the company. In 1928, Seatrain had introduced a service between Havana and U.S. East and Gulf Coast ports carrying rail freight cars for discharge directly to a rail terminal in Havana for movement over the Cuban rail system. It was the first known use of the roll on-roll off concept. (Source: *MARITIME ECONOMICS* by Martin Stopford) Decades later, after the revolution in Cuba and the subsequent virtual termination of U.S.-Cuba trade, these vessels were shifted to the Puerto Rican trade, even though Puerto Rico had no railroads.

In Edgewater, Bill Cole, the Container Division executive vice president, shared a corner office with Pack, their desks abutting each other, much like the arrangement Pack and Kahn had at their Manhattan headquarters, where the two shared an antique partner's desk, each facing the other. That first day, I took a seat in the Edgewater office waiting for Cole to arrive (Pack was there only on rare occasions), which he finally did at 10 a.m., his usual routine. He told me, "You'll be sharing the office adjacent to mine with John Arwood, our other senior vice president, and you will be responsible for our Caribbean Services." "Caribbean" meant Seatrain's Puerto Rican service, since the company had no other services in the region at the time.

I encountered many interesting characters during my time at Seatrain, and my office-mate, John Arwood, was one of them. An intense, redheaded (sometimes red-faced) southerner, he was slender, strongly built, and had played college football. His telephone speaking style was just short of shouting, which didn't do much to provide a relaxed working atmosphere. Even though we were totally different in most of our ways, we got along well. He was a pure operating type, having served in that capacity with Sea-Land (America's premier container line at the time), and was responsible for all our container-related activities, including the purchase of equipment, terminal operations, and the installation and operation of a computer system that would track our containers.

Arwood had a strong aversion to Bill Cole, telling me "If it ever comes to a showdown, I'll grab a piece of lumber and beat the hell out of him," an odd way to talk about one's boss. It eventually dawned on me that one of the reasons Cole had brought me on board was to act as a counterfoil to Arwood. As it happened, I was quickly given additional responsibilities while Arwood, regularly at odds with Cole, continued to be frustrated in carrying out his duties as he saw them. I kept waiting for the big showdown, but it never got to that point, and Arwood soon left the company. His career flourished once he was away from Cole, and he eventually became president of another shipping venture.

I quickly began to study the Puerto Rican trade route, which, under U.S. law, requires the exclusive use of American-built and -crewed vessels. I started by visiting our operations in Puerto Rico where I met the newly appointed manager, Roberto Guevarro, a handsome Puerto Rican, with dark, curly hair. Guevarro was tall and athletic, affable, and well-liked by our Puerto Rican customers and by the all-important local union leadership. We quickly became friends. Roberto had replaced Bill Gohlke, who had run afoul of Bill Cole, was removed from his post, and was transferred back to U.S. headquarters. There he languished with no specified duties or responsibilities until he was assigned to my office, a bitter man who undoubtedly felt he should have had my job.

In many respects, Gohlke had been a superb company representative in Puerto Rico. A Southerner, like Arwood, but without a college education, Gohlke had once been a truck driver. He was extremely shrewd and enormously energetic, and for him, Puerto Rico had become a virtual fiefdom. He was a lavish entertainer and a big gambler at the various local casinos. He boasted about his friendship with the entertainer Sammy Davis Jr., a frequent headliner at the El San Juan Hotel, one of Gohlke's favorite watering holes. He had close ties to many government officials, and excellent relations with some of our major customers. Even though he had been a key player in the early development of Sea-Land, he had been easily recruited by Seatrain, probably because he had displayed the same uncontrollable personality traits at Sea-Land that we saw when he came to work for us. Gohlke's problem was that at Seatrain, in Bill Cole's view, there was room for only one star: Bill Cole.

Our Puerto Rican service was losing money, principally because of high operating expenses. My first task was to terminate the carriage of loaded railroad cars to an island that had no railroads. I persuaded Cole, and Pack and Khan, to make alterations to our ships in the Puerto Rican service vessels so that they would carry only containers. Next, I addressed Seatrain's weak marketing and sales program by instituting a system of competitive statistics; by the reassignment of our sales representatives to make the most of their respective capabilities; and by the assignment of our major accounts directly to Bill Gohlke, whom I appointed vice president of sales, hoping to make use of his considerable talents.

The Federal Maritime Commission regulated freight rates in the Puerto Rican trade, and any change of rates required Commission approval. There was constant pressure by importers in Puerto Rico, strongly supported by the Puerto Rican government, to maintain freight rates at the lowest possible levels. This pressure, combined with fierce competition by the lines in the trade, Sea-Land, Seatrain, and Transamerican Trailer Transport, made the Puerto Rican service only marginally profitable. Unlike international trades where the conference system allowed member lines to join together to set rates, exempt from anti-trust laws, U.S. shipping law did not permit collaboration among carriers serving the Puerto Rican trade or in any other domestic trade route, including Hawaii, Alaska, and Guam. Because of these restrictions and the intense competition, it was virtually impossible to make an acceptable return on the capital invested.

I was, however, successful in expanding revenues in the Puerto Rican service by adding service to St. Thomas in the Virgin Islands, Santo Domingo, Haiti, and eventually Trinidad, using small foreign-flag feeder vessels, transferring containers to and from the mainline vessels at San Juan, the system pioneered by Sea-Land that had so effectively eliminated Grace Line from those trades. The concept was that since Puerto Rico alone did not generate sufficient volume, there was unused cargo space on the large mainline vessels, and only the actual out-of-pocket feeder-vessel charter hire and container-handling expenses to and from the feeders would be considered in determining profitability. I hired my old friend and former Grace Line compatriot, George Spiotta, to organize and run this niche operation.

The addition of our service to these ports led to some interesting experiences, particularly in Santo Domingo, where the 1961 assassination of General Rafael Trujillo, the country's dictator since 1930, led to some uneasy relationships with the new government, and where power now rested with the Dominican military. Early in 1972, based on Spiotta's

Bill Gohlke, Art, and Oscar Cohen celebrating new service to Santo Domingo,
LISTIN DIARIO, February 8, 1972

recommendation, we helped Oscar Cohen, operations manager with Grace Line's Dominican agents, to form a new agency company and assumed Seatrain's agency work. Cohen was a graduate of the Dominican maritime academy (their Kings Point) and had excellent relations with graduates of its naval academy (their Annapolis).

These included the Commodore of the Dominican Navy, who was credited with a major assist in the overthrow of the Trujillo government by taking his small fleet of war ships up the Ozama River and bombarding the Presidential Palace. Through Oscar's connections, Seatrain was in a favored position when seeking port facilities and overcoming local operating problems. To help cement this relationship, Cohen arranged a reception at his home, honoring the Commodore and senior members of his staff, which I attended.

Second from left, Roberto Guevarro, next, the Commodore, Art, Oscar Cohen, George Spiotta; Santo Domingo, Dominican Republic, 1972

*   *   *   *

In a company-wide memorandum dated July 17, 1970, Cole announced that I had been "promoted to Senior Vice-President – Marketing for all services for Seatrain Lines Container Division." This meant that in addition to the Caribbean Services, I must now reorganize marketing and sales for our new European service, and manage the introduction of the giant new high-speed Euro-class container vessels. After reviewing our efforts to date, and meeting with each of our sales representatives, I felt compelled to terminate and replace the managers in six of our key sales positions. I also initiated a sales concept new to our industry: corporate sales executives, each to work with the companies in a specific commodity sector, e.g., tobacco, chemicals, automotive. The objective was for these specialists to develop a broad, thorough understanding of their particular commodity and its major players.

To fill these new positions, I hired only proven salesmen, not necessarily those with maritime shipping experience, at executive salaries. Seatrain provided them several months' indoctrination in the fundamentals of our business. This approach worked well with the major accounts, as our "specialists" outsold the competition and, reporting directly to me, received close support from our customer service, pricing, and operating departments. I made it a point to accompany them at meetings and luncheons with their top customers. We developed competitive statistics, largely through securing cargo manifests from any source available, employing all the reporting systems essential to a well coordinated sales effort. We also established a network of sales offices and agents in the United States.

*   *   *   *

"I can't believe I'm here," I thought to myself, sitting in the spacious conference room of Seatrain's European general agents in Amsterdam, gazing through the large picture windows, so common in Holland, at a picturesque canal with a backdrop of quaint buildings, bathed in the late spring sunshine which was finally visiting the Netherlands. I had trouble concentrating on the operating and marketing plan proposals being presented to our group of Seatrain senior management. But I quickly realized, early in my first visit to Europe for Seatrain, that the use of a traditional agency representation could never be effective against our competitors, all of whom had offices in major cities throughout Europe. It was obvious to me that Seatrain Line needed to establish a presence in key markets in Holland, Germany, France, Belgium, Scandinavia, and the UK. To help develop and lead such an organization, we would need a general manager based in Europe, probably operating out of a regional headquarters office in Rotterdam, the main point of entry and exit for European containerized cargoes.

Several months later, word reached me that the executive who occupied such a position for Sea-Land, Neal Nunnelly, was unhappy with his situation there. At the time, we were operating out of an office in Rotterdam provided by our general agent. Contact was made with Nunnelly and a meeting arranged at the hotel where I usually stayed, the Rotterdam Hilton. I was waiting in my suite when he arrived. "Hi, I'm Neal Nunnelly," he said as he stepped through the door. We struck up a warm relationship immediately. I learned that his problem was with his boss. "He doesn't give me much leeway in managing the European operation, and keeps trying to micromanage from corporate headquarters in Newark." At dinner, we settled the terms of his employment and then took a walk around the town center, mingling with the crowds celebrating the Rotterdam victory in the

Art, second from left, then Neal

European Soccer Club championship match earlier in the day. Men were climbing telephone and streetlight poles, scrambling up the huge stone blocks of the Town Hall, yelling and cheering, and plenty of alcohol was flowing. That was my first encounter with the fan-mania surrounding the most popular sport in the world, the football Americans call soccer. Neal and I became fast friends as well as work associates. He was about my age, a bit shorter than I am, with a slender, sculptured build, wavy light brown hair, an etched Celtic face, and a great sense of humor. Together, we set up offices in Hamburg, London, Copenhagen, and, through an agent, in Paris.

Our manager in London and our representative in Paris were promoted from the corporate account executive sales staff I had organized earlier. In both Hamburg and Copenhagen we were able to recruit outstanding young executives from our competitors. Neal and I frequently visited these branch offices together. In London, after a long day with our local people, Neal would say, "Well, it's steam bath and massage time." "Yeah, let's move it," I'd reply. Then off we'd go to our favorite massage parlor, three blocks from the London Hilton where we usually stayed. Those were the great old days of hard travel, hard work, and occasional relaxation.

Art at center; at right, Klaus Behrens, General Manager, Germany

Seatrain maintained a two-bedroom flat in a ritzy apartment building in London. (One of the building's previous tenants had been Prime Minister Harold Wilson.) The flat was also made available to Seatrain customers visiting or passing through London, and served as an excellent marketing tool. Well stocked with liquor, it was often party time there for our clients. I did use the flat on occasion, particularly when Jeanette accompanied me.

My most interesting trips were to Poland, Czechoslovakia, Hungary, and Yugoslavia, all of them, of course, behind the Iron Curtain. We'd hire a six-passenger, propeller-driven airplane with a pilot and co-pilot, and make a round of visits to Warsaw, Prague, Budapest, and Belgrade, meeting with the state purchasing departments of these Soviet Bloc nations. I recall a dinner party in Warsaw, with officials from the Polish Ocean Line, at an elegant restaurant in the cellar of an old castle, drinking toasts of vodka. "Here's to the gallant Polish knights who fought the last great battle of mounted knights against the Teutonic Germans," one of the Poles exclaimed, adding, "We would never have won that battle without the help of the Bohemian army, who made a forced march from their homeland." Since I am of Czech descent and Czechoslovakia included the former Kingdom of Bohemia, this was obviously a gesture they made to help cement our relationship. As for business, we executed a contract whereby the Polish Ocean Line would feeder Seatrain containers between Hamburg and Gdynia, the principal Polish port on the Baltic. The evening ended with the two of us and our hosts en route to our hotel in a horse-drawn open buggy, all of us singing exuberantly as we finished off a bottle of wine.

On another occasion we were in Prague to conclude a contract with Czechofracht, the import-export arm of the Czech government, by which Seatrain was guaranteed a major share of all Czech cargoes moving to the United States. Final execution of the contract took place in the beer garden of the famous Pilsner Brewery just outside the city. As we toured the brewery, we were treated to draft Pilsner poured into large mugs, directly from the production line, "It's a pleasure to make an agreement with another Czech, even if he can't speak the language," commented the Czechofracht's general manager with a smile, as we downed our fourth mug of one of the world's greatest beers.

Nunnelly had laid the groundwork for this contract during a previous visit, when he convinced Viktor, the general manager's assistant, that Seatrain was the carrier that they should support. Neal told me his conversation with Viktor went something like this: "Nunnelly, you know that I really want to recommend your line, but you do have competitors who have been very helpful to me." "Well, Viktor," Nunnelly replied, "I consider you a good friend, and I'd like to express my goodwill." The two men were strolling through the old town, under the ancient cuckoo clock, which for a long time during the Cold War years hadn't worked. At the time, "golden" Prague wasn't so golden. All heating was by coal, and the city was a study in gray. Gray brick buildings were covered with gray coal dust, especially in the winter months, when even people's overcoats were gray or black. Viktor was wearing a worn gray coat and a battered black hat, and was clearly looking for something of value. On several occasions in the past he had admired Nunnelly's Rolex watch. "Well, old friend," Neal said, as he wrapped his arm around Viktor's narrow shoulders, "Clearly, your famous clock doesn't work. So the least I can do is provide you a timepiece." Then he unbuckled the gold strap of the beautiful watch and slipped it into the ready hand of the Czech bureaucrat. From that point forward, prompted by a gift now and then, having Viktor there was as good as having a local representative.

Budapest, with its wide multi-lane bridge across the Danube joining the separate cities of Buda and Pest, was considerably more attractive than Prague. We were warmly greeted there, lodged in the best hotel, and well entertained on our first visit to negotiate a contract for the movement of hundreds of trucks from the U.S. to Hungary. "How do you like our famous wines?" one of our hosts asked as we were treated to an excellent meal in the finest restaurant in Budapest, in a converted palace of the old kings of Hungary. "Good, good!" I exclaimed as we proceeded to make our deal. But when we returned months later to negotiate the settlement of a substantial claim for damage to the trucks, allegedly incurred while they were transported by Seatrain Line, it was a different matter that quickly became clear when we arrived at our hotel. Our rooms faced a weed-strewn courtyard, with a single naked light bulb hanging from each room's stained ceiling, and a communal bathroom with filthy toilets and rusted plumbing. We were dealing with hard-eyed Hungarian government bureaucrats who wouldn't give an inch, and we did not agree on a settlement No dinners and no wine; just back to the dump where we stayed, a quick meal in the hotel's dilapidated cafe, and so to bed, trying to sleep, as the paper-thin walls allowed every sort of sound to penetrate and mix with an assortment of unrecognizable aromas. The next morning, after a meager, tasteless breakfast, we were off to another day of acrimonious, unsuccessful discussions. "Thank God we got out of the country in one piece," remarked Nunnelly as we boarded our small plane. I don't remember if the claim was ever settled, but it was tough for the Hungarians to force a settlement since we had already collected the freight charges.

Belgrade was the most westernized of the lot, since Marshal Tito had managed to avoid most of the ham-handed restrictions imposed by the Soviets. There were shops carrying an array of imported goods, lively restaurants and bars, and the sidewalks in the old town were busy with strolling locals. Tito encouraged privately-owned businesses, and we were therefore able to employ a local agency company to represent us. We met with the president of the agency in his office, a comfortable room with prewar upholstered chairs and an antique desk. He was a stocky, older man with a weathered face, a graying beard, and pale brown eyes. A large framed photo of Tito was hanging on the wall behind his desk. He was proud of the fact that he had served with Tito in the partisan forces during the war, and I was duly impressed when he said, "Tito is a close friend of mine. We are both Serbs and fought side by side." We found it easy to do business in Yugoslavia, especially with an ex-partisan looking after our interests, and were completely unaware that the country was a smoldering cauldron of small Balkan states held together under Tito's iron fist.

One of my most interesting trips was to Tehran, the capital of Iran, which I visited by myself in 1972 to assess the extent of the backlog of containers (on chassis being pulled by German trucks) waiting to be cleared for entry into the country. These units had moved through the port of Hamburg, then overland to Iran, and several thousand of them, from various steamship lines, had been stalled for weeks awaiting clearance by the notoriously inefficient Iranian customs service. I arrived at my hotel late in the evening, having made a reservation through our agents. I was exhausted from travel, and surprised at the number of people stretched out on the lounge chairs and lying on the lobby rug, trying to sleep. At that time, Iran was ruled by the Shah and was open for business with Western nations, bringing many eager visitors. There was simply not enough hotel space, and I had visions of staking a claim to some part of the lobby floor. "I'm sorry," said the desk clerk, "but we have no reservation for you." I was staring bleary-eyed at the counter in front of him, and responded, "Well why is my name listed on that piece of paper?" leaning over the counter and pointing. After a good deal of argument, I was assigned a room. I realize now that it would have been much easier if I had just slipped him some money, which was, not surprisingly, the custom there.

The next day, our agents drove me to the area where hundreds of containers were stretched in lines as far as the eye could see, waiting to be emptied of their cargoes, a very costly situation for the shipping lines which needed this equipment to move cargoes back to the U.S., but our agents convinced me that they were doing all they could to expedite clearance by Iranian customs authorities. We met that evening at a typical Iranian restaurant to enjoy some fine local cuisine, occasionally smoking from the water pipes there. "Yes," one of them said, "Iran is very fortunate, with the Shah firmly in place. We are a good country for you Americans to do business in." I wonder what he would say if he were alive today.

Art on far left trying out his water pipe, with Seatrain Line Agents, Teheran, Iran, 1972

*   *   *   *

Chapter 7

SEATRAIN LINE ROUND TWO

I have explained in previous chapters that steamship lines serving a U.S trade lane could form a "conference" whose purpose was to set a common or uniform level of freight rates or charges, and, with the approval of the Federal Maritime Commission, such conferences would be exempt from U.S. antitrust laws. But the changes forced on the established carriers in the North Atlantic trades by Sea-Land -- the transition from breakbulk to containerized cargoes -- and the entry into the trade of Seatrain's larger and faster new containerships, resulted in chaotic competitive conditions. The conference system was proving vulnerable, and reducing freight rates to repulse the "upstart" Seatrain became a common practice among the conference carriers. Seatrain had rapidly carved out a significant slice of the market, largely through rate reductions backed by excellent service. The financial impact on the conference lines was devastating, and they realized that it was essential to their survival to persuade Seatrain to join the North Atlantic conferences.

The conference carriers which had been in the North Atlantic trades for many years, some of them more than a century, were United States Line (U.S.), Hapag Lloyd (German), Dart (Belgian), American Export (U.S.), and Atlantic Container Line (a combination of several well known carriers such as Cunard and the Swedish-American Line), thoroughly disliked Seatrain and its operations. But their survival required practical solutions, and the ultimate anti-competitive device, sharing the total combined revenues of all the carriers on an agreed percentage basis, was doggedly pursued in a concerted effort by the conference carriers in repeated meetings with Seatrain Line. Seatrain was well aware that this provided a promising opportunity, depending on the share allocated to them. But Federal Maritime Commission approval of such an anti-competitive device was absolutely essential. Inevitably, reaching an agreement on the percentage to be assigned to each carrier proved a daunting task.

A number of high-level executive meetings were held, many of them in Europe so as to be outside of U.S. territory, yet the feisty, hands-on FMC Chairman at the time, Helen Delich Bentley, arguably the best ever to hold that position, closely monitored the proceedings. Finally, after exhausting round-the-clock negotiations, an agreement among the lines was reached as to the share of total revenues to be allotted to each participating carrier, and Seatrain secured a percentage exceeding its actual performance up to that point. But imagine an arrangement wherein competing carriers could collude in setting freight-rate levels without fear of antitrust laws, while being guaranteed a specific share of total revenues and allowed to provide vessel space to match projected movements, thus avoiding the cost that comes from unused vessel space. In the end, the Maritime Commission, showing good sense in protecting the importers and exporters and therefore the consumer, refused to approve the agreement.

While I had been personally active in the shipping conferences in which Grace had participated, primarily in the Caribbean and South American trades, I was now thrown into the big leagues: the U.S.-European trades were easily the largest of them all. There was an interesting assortment of senior executives representing the competition. Karl-Heinz Sager of Hapag-Lloyd looked like one of those blond Teutonic SS troopers who in Hollywood movies peer from a tank turret during World War II. He spoke excellent English and was serious and articulate, but he could also be distant and arrogant. In his irreverent way, Mike Diaz, my former boss at Grace Line, now President of American Export, occasionally reminded Karl, "Just remember who won the war." Some years later, Sager went on to found Senator Line, a new global containership line, and appointed Mike Diaz as head of the line's U.S. operations.

Then there was Paul Richardson, President of Sea-Land, the carrier founded by Malcom McLean and generally recognized as the most innovative and fastest-growing of all the major container lines. Paul was the most charming of all the company executives: a wiry, curly-haired, handsome man, Irish in appearance with his blue eyes and ruddy complexion. Paul was about my age, and spoke with a distinctive Boston accent as befits a Massachusetts son. His loud, spontaneous laugh could be heard often since he enjoyed the telling of a good story. Before joining Sea-Land, he had been a trucking company salesman, and was now the charismatic head of what would become one of the two largest containership lines in the world, the other being Maersk Line, the Danish-owned carrier which had not yet entered the Atlantic trades. All the senior Sea-Land executives were former truckers, like McLean, and were not always comfortable in the company of those executives who had made the transition from breakbulk to container shipping. I was, of course, the new guy on the block with all of them, and it took some time to break the ice.

Another interesting study was the CEO of Atlantic Container Line, Philip Bates, a condescending Brit with sandy brown hair and a reddish face who occasionally addressed me as "Old Boy." Before the formation of ACL, a combination of long-established carriers joined to cope with the container age, he had worked for one of them, Cunard Line, for many years. Once I was his guest at dinner at his venerable club in London, one that featured traditional leather couches, mahogany paneling, worn rugs, and family coats-of-arms on the walls. While enjoying our after-dinner Port, a regular Bates indulgence, he introduced me to the club manager, who, as it happened, had served in the British Army during the war as an enlisted man under Bates, an officer. Master and servant, persisting in their relationship: to me, in a way, this was an example of the English class system. Bates, as with many others in the trade, was doing his best to understand what Seatrain was all about. On the other hand, the Americans, Mike Diaz of American Export and Ed Heine (a Kings Pointer and lawyer), president of U.S. Lines, were easy to work with and understood well enough that Seatrain was the fox in the henhouse.

I received my first taste of the career bureaucrats who served as executive directors for the European-based steamship conferences when I attended the initial meeting of one of the conferences in London. I walked into the conference room a bit early for the meeting and spied a gentleman with thinning brown hair and a stiff posture, appearing much like an English butler in a British film. Hoping to establish a relationship, I decided to sit next to him. After a long silence, he finally looked up from his morning *London Times* and said, "So you're the new Seatrain man. Have you been to London before?" I wasn't sure whether this was a wisecrack or an honest inquiry, but I answered, "Yes, several times," whereupon he said "Oh?" and went back to reading his newspaper. It seemed that no one was fond of the upstarts who dared challenge the established order in the Atlantic trades.

The senior representatives of the member lines met regularly at various pricey hotels and resorts, primarily in Europe, in places like Warnemunde, London, Lisbon, Hamburg, and Paris. One of the attractions of these special executive meetings was that we could bring our wives and socialize with other couples in the evenings. Neal Nunnelly, Seatrain's European manager, usually accompanied me and added some spice to the routine, such as an interesting experience we had together while in Warnemunde, this time without our wives. After a long workday of negotiations and debate, I suggested to Neal, "Let's go have a swim," knowing that the hotel had two large indoor pools. After renting bathing suits, we changed in the locker room and then proceeded to the nearest of the two pools, with a number of men and women already in the water, and dove in. Upon surfacing, we heard the lifeguard shout something in German, and, realizing that we didn't understand him, then in English, "You can't swim here in a bathing suit!" It was a nude-only pool. Neal responded, "Sounds good to me, we need some underwater practice anyway," so it was off with the bathing suits and into the pool, diving deep, with our eyes wide open.

Even with the immunity the steamship conferences had from U.S. antitrust laws, the members still thought they needed additional advantages in competing with one another, and resorted to such illegal practices as subsidizing inland trucking, misnaming commodities being shipped in order to secure lower freight rates, and, the most flagrant of all, outright rebating. The lines had apparently been engaging in these in these practices for some time, and Seatrain was not slow to catch on. Deals were usually negotiated in Europe, with some of the major chemical companies in Germany even establishing small departments in their companies for the sole purpose of keeping track of

111

rebates owed them by the carriers that handled their shipments. So, in keeping with established practice, Seatrain set up a special bank account in Switzerland to be used for that purpose. Eventually, these activities led to a major investigation by the Federal Maritime Commission. By that time, I had left the company, but Neal Nunnelly was subpoenaed after he too had left Seatrain (a story in itself, to which I will revert later in this narrative). Eventually, all the North Atlantic Lines were hit with substantial fines.

I traveled routinely in Europe, primarily to coordinate Seatrain's marketing efforts. Sometimes Jeanette accompanied me. I recall our first trip together to Paris. We arrived at the airport, tired and disheveled after an overnight flight, and proceeded to the Hilton Hotel where we had reserved a room, only to learn that we couldn't check-in until 3 p.m. At the time, I did not know this was a common practice. Outraged at the thought of sitting around the hotel lobby for six hours, I huffily grabbed our bags and hustled Jeanette out to the curbside where we hailed a taxi. "Can you recommend a hotel?" I said to the cab driver. "Oui," said he, and off we went. About twenty minutes later, we were ushered into the quiet and unassuming lobby of an old hotel, where all that was available

Art, Jeanette and Jim Davis, Seatrain Paris Representative; Arc de Triumph in background

was a suite. I turned to Jeanette and said, "What the heck, let's do it." Once inside the suite, Jeannette exclaimed, "Wow, look at the size of the bedroom. Can you believe a complete living room, and get a gander at the powder room, just for me." I later learned that the *George V* was one of the finest hotels in Paris, a fact further confirmed on checking out a week later when we reviewed the bill.

One evening, joined by our local representative, Jim Davis, we dined with Jack Jackson, the international traffic director of the DuPont Company, one of our major customers, who was in Paris on business. Before being assigned to Paris, Davis had been the Seatrain sales executive responsible for our business with chemical companies, working out of our corporate office, and we both knew Jackson quite well. He stood ramrod straight, had thinning hair and a long, alert and finely featured face. He was also used to having carriers like Seatrain fawn upon him. I well recall that after dinner in a superb, expensive restaurant, we were invited to visit the basement wine cellar. It was crammed with endless rows of the finest wines, all gathering dust, and I thoughtfully suggested to our guest, "Jack, would you like a bottle?" Without skipping a beat, he plucked one from the rack in front of him. The bottle looked as if it had been there for a score of years, and so it had. Vintage 1950, priced at about $150. I was hoping that he would treat this costly item with respect; but, while we walked back to his hotel, he began to juggle the Chateau Rothschild Pinot Noir like a bowling pin, tossing it into the air and expertly catching it by the neck after each spin.

*   *   *   *

Seatrain proved a tough competitor in the Atlantic trades with the newest, largest and fastest vessels; a large pool of new containers; poised to achieve a global reach enabling it to move containers to and from most points in the U.S., the Caribbean, Europe, the Far East, and Hawaii. These newly constructed European service ships were designated *Euro* class and were named *Euroliner, Eurofreighter, Asialiner,* and *Asiafreighter.* The two last-named ships were originally scheduled to enter the newly established Far East service, thus their names, but were assigned to the European trades owing to the rapidly escalating demand for container cargo space in the North Atlantic routes, a demand that Seatrain could not satisfy with only two vessels.

The *Euro* class were the only gas turbine-powered commercial vessels in the world. (U.S. Navy aircraft carriers were also gas turbine-powered.) They could cruise at an astonishing 27 knots and make the transatlantic crossing in five and a half days. Each

113

ship provided a thousand 40-foot container spaces. At that time, the competition was operating 20-knot vessels with a capacity of about 750 40-foot containers. Seatrain's container pool numbered 23,000, primarily 40-foot vans (the standard length for over-the-road trailers in the U.S.), but also high-cube containers (going from the norm of 8 feet in height to 8½ feet); open-top (for handling odd sized cargoes); insulated (for cargoes that needed protection from cold weather, such as beverages); refrigerated (for temperature-sensitive cargo like fruit, or frozen fish) tank containers to transport all types of liquids, flats and car carriers.

One day while sitting in my office I thought to myself, "Passenger vessels vie for an award called the "Blue Ribbon" for the fastest time across the Atlantic. At the time, the record was held by the *United States,* which reportedly could exceed 30 knots when used as a naval auxiliary in time of war. "Why not a blue ribbon for commercial cargo ships?" So I decided on the spur of the moment that we would create such an award and give it to ourselves. Out went a press release, "Seatrain Captures Blue Ribbon!" with a picture of an award ceremony showing me holding a silver cup citing the *Eurofreighter* for capturing the trans-Atlantic speed record, with a crossing speed averaging 27.1 knots.

Further positive publicity was garnered by our announcement of the move of all Seatrain Line staff from Edgewater to the company's newly constructed headquarters office in Weehawken. Sited on the landside adjacent to its recently-completed container terminal, the building had an all-glass exterior and a large central atrium where modern artwork and sculptures were exhibited, It contained three floors of modern offices, all with outside views. Howard Pack maintained a large corner office on the second floor, overlooking the terminal, and my office was next to his. He used the office just a few days a month, but when he did, he could be a royal pain. "Art, I've been counting how many container moves our gantries make an hour, and over two hours it was an average of about twenty -- doesn't seem like enough. Can't we improve on it?" Of course we could. Only a few years later, the norm would be about thirty moves an hour. But my mind was on other things, and I don't remember how I responded to him.

Make no mistake about it, Seatrain's owners, Howard Pack and Joe Khan, were true visionaries, aiming from the start for a grand slam with their container venture: market leadership by innovative technology, massive injection of hardware, superior management, and ruthless capital input. They were confident that high earnings from the tanker and charter segments would carry the Container Division until it could find its own way. As the President of the Container Division, I was the guy who was supposed to make this happen. It was a gigantic task, becoming more complicated every day as Seatrain added new services and the organization necessary to support global expansion.

In eighteen months, the Container Division opened regional offices in thirty European ports and hinterland cities, not only to serve the needs of vessel port calls, but also to back up the sales efforts of its European headquarters staff in Rotterdam and at the UK base in London. A similar sales organization was rapidly developed in the United States and Canada. Chartered vessels would be used in the Europe-U.S. West Coast service,

Eurofreighter alongside the Weehawken terminal

which complemented the East Coast service. I remember having lunch in Manhattan with Pack and Kahn one day. Pack asked me, "What do you think about starting a West Coast service with three small vessels?" "I'm not sure, there's tough competition already in place," I replied. Kahn joined in with, "Come on Art, I know you can do it. We've got to make our move now. After all, we can charter these vessels at a very low rate." So that was it.

An Aeromarine shot of *Plutos* on trials off the Hook of Holland

Seatrain also added a Europe-U.S. Gulf service, again with chartered tonnage; this was closely followed by a trans-Pacific service, also with chartered ships. Then

Pacific service: *Spindrift Isle*

came the biggest innovation of all, a transcontinental container on rail flatcar service joining the East and Gulf coasts with West Coast ports, to be known as "landbridge." Such a service would allow containers to be moved from one coast to the other, eliminating the need for vessels to make a Panama Canal transit. For example, on the movement of a container from Rotterdam to Los Angeles, instead of the containership's having to transit the Canal, the container could be offloaded in New York and moved by rail to Los Angeles. I had picked up on this idea and passed it on to Pack and Khan, recommending it. They responded to my suggestion, which was based on extensive studies of rail costs and countless meetings with railroad executives, with "Let's do it," and we immediately set out to convince the railroads that the landbridge concept would be a winner.

Executive vice president of Penn Central RR and Art at New Jersey rail yard with first landbridge train, 1972

The system required connections between the Atchison Topeka and Santa Fe/Penn Central, the Erie Lackawanna, and the Southern Pacific. To accomplish this, Seatrain leased two trains, one complete train weekly each way, made up of 60 flatcars, each carrying two of the line's 40-foot containers. Today, nearly everyone has seen these long landbridge trains; but Seatrain was the carrier whose owners had the foresight to initiate the service when most transportation executives said it wouldn't work. Landbridge charges covered the move from point of origin to port of loading, thence by ocean carrier, transfer to rail cars at ports of entry, movement across the U.S., and finally delivery from the rail yard to the consignee. Rates were competitive with all-water rates; and total in-transit times, door-to-door, averaged a week less than all-water transit via the Panama Canal, a major inducement to the shipper.

I well remember the day in 1972 when we christened the first landbridge train, breaking a bottle of champagne over the front of the Penn Central locomotive.

Art's secretary about to christen the first landbridge train across the United States, 1972

Such ship-rail systems soon acquired the name "intermodal" and for us at Seatrain it was an intermodal dream come true to see this train stretching for almost a mile, carrying only Seatrain containers.

By that time, Bill Cole had left the company, and I succeeded him as president of the container division. Cole had become uncomfortable with the fast pace and complexities generated by the demands of the container revolution. His background was in chartering, matching ships with full cargoes. In December, 1971, Howard Pack announced that Frank Troxel, President of Seatrain California, would report to me in order to improve coordination of Seatrain's worldwide container system. As a result, I was thrust into the Far East and Hawaiian trades. Troxel had spearheaded Seatrain's start-up growth in the Pacific and was probably not too happy about this new reporting relationship.

I worked hard to gain his trust and confidence, primarily by refraining from involvement in his day-to-day operations, assuming a coordinating role and focusing on overall strategy.

Troxel had previously worked for twelve years with Matson Line and was a well-respected executive there. Matson Line was a subsidiary of Alexander Baldwin and Company, a long-established landowner with vast holdings in Hawaii and the primary Hawaiian producer of pineapples. Baldwin had dominated the Hawaiian trade for more than a century. It must have been a shock to Matson when Seatrain built its own container terminal in Honolulu, right under their eyes. With Frank's guidance, the service was well-accepted by the time I visited the Seatrain operation in Honolulu with him. I was impressed by his close working relations with the major importers on those beautiful islands, most of whose needs were supplied from the U.S. mainland. We were marketing types and eventually meshed very well together. He had reddish hair and a craggy face that broke out in frequent smiles. Wiry and muscular, his preferred attire was cowboy boots and a Western style shirt which he wore while taking spins on his Harley over the winding roads north of the Golden Gate Bridge. "This is what relieves my tension, and I'd recommend it." "No way," I thought to myself.

In preparation for the introduction of Seatrain's new Far East service, Frank and I traveled together to various points in the Orient. In Tokyo, in company with our agents, Dodwell & Co., a long established British-owned agency company, we met with the Japanese Electronic Exporters Association to seek their support in acquiring a share of Japan's huge electronics export trade with the United States. This was our first experience in negotiating with a group of powerful exporters who did business in Japanese fashion. Even after being coached by our agents, we were still edgy when the members of the association filed silently into the large conference room. I greeted these potential customers warmly and went directly into our presentation, starting out with something like: "We are very pleased that you have agreed to meet with us today. We believe we can provide excellent service at considerable savings in costs." I went on to outline the kind of service we planned, including its frequency and port coverage, and presented a proposal that would oblige them to commit a substantial volume of their exports to Seatrain in order to achieve any significant reduction in freight charges.

We waited expectantly for a response. They sat quietly for a few minutes, saying nothing, finally asking for a break to allow them to caucus. In thirty minutes they returned and once again sat quietly, without expression. At last, their spokesman, the Sony representative, offered, "Ah yes, very interesting proposal, we must study further before replying." We hadn't fully appreciated the significance of their close ties to the Japanese carriers N.Y.K, Mitsui, K-Line, and several others. These lines were subsidiaries or affiliates of the powerful business mergers controlled by wealthy families, called *Zaibatsu*. Before and during World War II the Zaibatsu essentially controlled the coal, steam engine, pulp, and aluminum industries and since then have acquired even greater economic power by expanding into shipping, banking and other industries. The greatest of these families were the Mitsui, Iwasaki (operating under the company name Mitsubishi), Sumitomo, and Yasuda. (Source: Volume 14, *FUNK & WAGNALL NEW ENCYCLOPEDIA*). Seatrain was an unknown and untried carrier hoping to secure commitments for large blocks of cargo to support our forthcoming service. The answer was an inevitable: "No. We must wait to test your service." Eventually, we did get some of their business.

Frank Troxel and Art visiting the Seatrain agents in Taiwan (note the picture of Chiang Kai-shek)

Frank and I also made regular visits to Seatrain's agents in Korea, Taiwan, and Hong Kong, all served by smaller feeder ships that transshipped containers at the port of Yokohama. We gradually learned the customs and business practices of the Orient, helped in great measure by Jim Hori ("Jim" was our version of his first name), a Japanese national we had hired as our special representative. Jim spoke excellent English, with an American accent. He had been educated in the U.S. and seemed torn between the two cultures, but he had important contacts in the region, and was able to expedite our programs for rapid growth. He was taller than most Japanese men, well built, with classic Oriental features, gregarious, yet with a certain aloofness. It was Jim who took me to a country hotel for a weekend, a traditional Japanese structure, with large airy suites, with bamboo dividers separating the several rooms. He insisted I try a massage. I had visions of a lovely Japanese girl in a loose-fitting kimono, but instead a wizened old blind man shuffled into my room. As he assaulted my back muscles, his fingers were like iron. Jim told me later that in Japan many of the practitioners of this ancient profession were blind. That night, we slept on soft pallets laid directly on the floor, with shaped wooden headrests. The next day, I was the only non-Japanese among a dozen naked men and women soaking in the hotel's hot sulfur springs.

Jim also took me on my only skiing expedition in Japan. He picked me up at my hotel on a Saturday morning, and it took us three hours to negotiate the heavy Tokyo traffic and reach the tunnel under a mountain and then on to the skiing area beyond. Our car was required to have chains wrapped around the rear wheels, which was accomplished at a way station prior to our proceeding further through the snow. I didn't have proper clothing, skis, or boots. The director of skiing was a large man for a Japanese, and, as a friend of Jim's, he let me borrow a ski jacket and pants, both of which were several sizes too small. His boots proved far too small and it took both Jim and me to squeeze my feet into them. I tried my first run. My toes were so cramped my feet began to freeze, and so that was it for skiing. I was the only non-Japanese staying at the skiing resort. The food was rural Japanese, which was fine with me, as I had grown very fond of typical Japanese cuisine.

Jim did produce some business opportunities, as witness the success Seatrain had in entering the Korean trade. It was my first trip to Seoul. The small restaurant was tucked into a corner of a narrow dead-end street, lined by one- and two-story wooden structures with ground-floor shops. Jim and I arrived at noon, as scheduled, ducking through a door only about five feet high, and adjusting our eyes to an interior dimly lit by a few scattered lamps. We were shown to a private enclosure where we sank to the floor onto thick mats, no problem for Jim, who made himself comfortable, legs crossed yoga style, while I began a series of adjustments of my long legs, finally thrusting them straight out on the floor. After a few minutes, a short Korean, indistinguishable from the men I had seen earlier that morning hurrying down the crowded sidewalks on their way to work, entered and greeted us with the customary bow and took a seat.

Mr. Kim Woo Choong was no typical businessman. The Daewoo Group, which he founded in 1967, would become one of the Big Four "Chaebol" (similar to the "Zaibatsu" in Japan) in South Korea. An industrial and multi-faceted service conglomerate, Daewoo was prominent in expanding its global market through joint ventures all over the world. The company initially concentrated on labor-intensive clothing and textile industries that provided high profit margins. Daewoo expanded into many other industries, including world-class shipyards, and became the sixth largest car manufacturer in the world. (Source: Internet website, http://en.wikipedia.org/wiki/Daewoo). All of these future developments were, of course, unknown to me at the time. "Well, Jim, it's nice to see you again," he stated in impeccable English. "I assume this is Mr. Novacek?" Jim had visited Kim in his office about a month earlier, in an effort to secure a share of the Daewoo shipments of textiles to the United States. Daewoo was moving twenty to thirty containers each week to the United States, the cargo we wanted for Seatrain to use as a base for a new service we were planning, connecting the port of Pusan, South Korea, with Yokohama by feeder vessel for transfer to Seatrain's mainline vessels. Jim and I had developed a plan, and now was the time to spring it on Kim. Of course, this was after we chatted about my impressions of Seoul and had ordered typical Korean dishes for our lunch, which included kimchi, fermented cabbage that had been stored underground, tasty, but with a stronger odor than garlic.

Always the entrepreneur, Kim asked, "So, what do you think Seatrain can do for me? There are plenty of containership services available." He was correct. There were already three or four similar services provided by the major Japanese, American, and European lines, although, at the time, Korea had no international shipping lines of its own. Jim explained our proposal: "We suggest you set up a steamship agency company to represent Seatrain in Korea. The port agency work is simple enough, and your own cargo movements would be a good base for other business. You would, of course, receive the usual agency commission on all cargoes moving on Seatrain bottoms to and from Korea." It didn't take Kim long to figure out he would be getting a five percent commission on moving his own cargo with Seatrain, an attractive and legal process.

In 1974, upon returning from a conference in Madrid, I received a call from Howard Pack, asking me to join him for lunch. Contrary to his usual upbeat attitude, he seemed a bit somber as we completed our meal. "Art, you've done a fine job in marketing our container services, but we feel we need to give closer attention to cost control. We're bringing in a new CEO for the Container Division, but want you to stay on and head up our marketing activities, as senior vice president of marketing. I'm sure you'll like the man we're bringing in. He previously served as president of a trucking company, where he was particularly effective in cutting costs." I was flabbergasted, and it took some time for me to digest this news. Looking back on it now, I realize that Seatrain had grown so fast that I was compelled to travel the world to introduce and market our many new services. What Pack was saying was probably true, but in my mind his was not the correct approach. It would have been better to bring in a chief operating officer, reporting to me, with the needed financial skills.

I probably should have quit the company immediately, but through some possibly misplaced loyalty I elected to stay on to assist the new man, and to see how things worked out. Of course, there was also the fact that there was no other job waiting for me, and I still had a large family to support. A day or two later, my replacement -- let's call him Joe – trooped in with several members of his trucking management team, arriving as replacements for our top-level operations and equipment control managers, both of whom departed as soon as they could find employment elsewhere.

Joe had no experience in international shipping, which, of course, included the container liner business. He was a nice enough guy, but came across as uncomfortable and tense, with the toughness you'd need to drive a big rig across the country. On our first trip to Rotterdam to visit our headquarters office, we were in adjacent hotel rooms and I overheard him in a phone conversation with his wife, literally shouting, as though an overseas call required it, "This is really something. Most every one of our employees in Europe speaks a foreign language and Holland is so different."

Art, far left, "Joe" far right

I learned that he had never been overseas before, other than for a stint in the armed forces building airstrips in Burma. It was painful and somewhat embarrassing to travel with him, not only because of his lack of knowledge of the industry, but also because of the looks of sympathy I received from my friends and business associates.

I guess I was in denial about the situation and really believed that things would work out for the better, which in a sense did happen for me, if not for the company. I even executed an extension of my employment agreement with Seatrain. I tried my best to help Joe, but it seemed quite difficult for him to make the transition to our industry; which is not to say that truckers couldn't be successful there.

As related in a previous chapter, Sea-Land, not to be confused with Seatrain, had been established some ten years earlier by Malcom McLean, who came from the trucking industry himself, and is largely recognized as the father of containerization. Joe had never been an owner of any company, never mind trucking, nor was he an entrepreneur. He had served as general manager of a mid-sized trucking company in the Midwest, and probably did very well at it, but I did not view him as a particularly good manager in Seatrain's situation. I found it amusing when he talked of "parking" a ship, rather than a traditional term "tying-up" or "mooring." Joe had no contacts in the maritime industry, and the trucking executives he brought into the company proved completely inept in dealing with the unique requirements of the rapidly changing containership business. Employee morale went to hell, and all of Seatrain's senior executives, except Neal Nunnelly, the general manager in Europe who stayed on for another year, promptly left the company. Joe's employment at Seatrain lasted about a year, when, by mutual agreement, he left.

At that point, Pack and Khan brought in another Container Division president. Let's call him Steve. I was not aware of it at the time, but I later learned that Pack and Khan were planning to sell the Container Division, and Steve was probably selected for the president's position, and also appointed an officer of the parent company because of his financial acumen. Furthermore, it was probably obvious to the owners that I was thoroughly disillusioned with the company and not a good choice to go back to my old job. Steve had been a senior executive at the Hertz Corporation, the car-rental service, and he brought in several of his associates from Hertz, who replaced Joe's trucking crew.

It seemed as if one group walked in while the other was walking out, and there I was again, introducing the new cast of characters to our organization. In the meantime, I continued in my marketing job, feeling helpless as I watched business drift away because of the disarray in our organization and services.

Art and "Steve"

Steve split his time between the Pack and Kahn offices in Manhattan and the Seatrain offices in Weehawken. His specialty was financial wheeling and dealing, and he was apparently good at it.

In late 1976, the Federal Maritime Commission advised Seatrain that it planned to conduct an extensive audit of Seatrain's operations. The completed audit documented what the FMC described as "numerous rebating practices," which were then reported to the Commission's Bureau of Enforcement. In turn, the Commission announced on September 19, 1978, that it had imposed a $2.5 million penalty on Seatrain Lines Inc. I found some comfort in the fact that Sea-Land and United States Lines had been fined for the same reasons. (I had resigned from Seatrain in February 1976 and was not directly involved in this matter.) My old friend, Neal Nunnelly, Seatrain's general manager in Europe, had been subpoenaed, and in an e-mail he sent me in 2004, nearly 30 years later, he wrote:

grouping.

9/9/78

FMC Penalizes Seatrain $2.5 Million for Rebating

Journal of Commerce Staff
WASHINGTON — The Federal Maritime Commission has announced it has imposed a $2.5 million penalty on Seatrain Lines Inc. for rebating practices.

This is the second largest civil penalty settlement in the history of the agency and represents the fourth settlement agreement reached between the FMC and an ocean carrier as part of its efforts to end rebating the ocean trades.

Seatrain was first contacted by the commission in 1976 and asked to complete an extensive audit of its operations. The carrier documented what the agency describes as "numerous rebating practices," which were reported to the FMC Bureau of Enforcement.

Under the Shipping Act of 1916, all common carriers in the U.S. ocean trades, whether U.S. of foreign, must file with the FMC and publish a tariff setting forth rates for transporting ocean cargo in the foreign trades of the U.S. The carriers must not depart from the published rates by rebating or offering other inducements to attract business.

In addition to the $2.5 million penalty, Seatrain has agreed to keep documents and audit data relating to the rebating and to make them available to the Commission. Seatrain has also agreed to initiate new procedures and periodic audits with a aim of any recurring malpractices. The settlement also includes a requirement that Seatrain pay to the FMC any money returned to it by recipients of the rebates.

Other carriers which have been penalized for rebating by the Commission are: Sea-Land Services, Inc., Blue Sea Lines and United States Lines. A settlement was also reached in a U.S. District Court action against Trans-Mex Lines for rebate payments in the U.S.-Spanish trade.

Also, 31 shippers have entered into settlement agreements totaling over $1 million. U.S. District Court actions have been filed against four shippers and one carrier which have refused to cooperate in the FMC's enforcement activities, the agency reports.

During this period, there were four or five occasions where a big black Mercedes from the US Embassy would drive to my house in Wassenaar and present subpoenas, compliments of Federal Grand Juries in remote places such as NY, NJ, and Ohio. Finally, the government realized that it wasn't just the hated Seatrain, but the whole bunch, and solved the problem by giving all a slap on the wrist and telling them not to do it again.

Neal's story goes much deeper. Shortly after I left Seatrain, he reportedly got into a serious disagreement with Steve over his employment contract with the company. I am uncertain about the issues involved, but do know that Neal felt he was being treated unfairly. He was also the only one at Seatrain trusted with the number of the Swiss bank account that allegedly funded special arrangements with its European customers. In any event, Nunnelly chose to leave Seatrain Line with no announcement being made, and literally dropped out of sight. Years later, a mutual friend told me that while he was Sydney, Australia, about ten years after Neal left Seatrain, he heard that Neal was on his yacht in Sydney Harbor.

"Art, you should have seen it. The yacht was about 70 feet long, and there was Neal sitting on deck in a white yachting outfit, accompanied by a beautiful Australian girl." He went on to advise me that Nunnelly had spent a number of years sailing the South Pacific, visiting the places where he had seen action while in the Navy during World War II. His wife had died of cancer, and he was pretty much free to go where he liked and do as he pleased. When Neal and I first reconnected by phone several years ago, he told me that he and his long-time companion still lived on the yacht, now permanently berthed in the San Francisco area.

Earlier I described the workings of the Steamship Conference system, and the many executive meetings that I attended over a period of years to deal with mutual pricing problems affecting the member lines. At all these meetings, attorneys representing lines as well as the conferences involved, were present, to make sure that there were no violations of anti-trust laws. The conference attorney was Hal Levy, another Kings Pointer, conscientious in representing the conferences, a difficult task in the face of pressure by his principals to accommodate their business interests. Hal was a close personal friend of several of the senior executives, particularly Mike Diaz, and, attending and socializing at most of the executive meetings, he may have found it difficult at times to insist on following the rules of the law. A native of Brooklyn with the hint of an accent to prove it, he had struggled financially to make his way through law school, and had an uncanny knowledge of the laws governing our industry, always willing to take as much time as was allowed him to express his legal opinions. Smart and quick witted, he would become a close friend.

Two years after I resigned from Seatrain, I received an unnerving letter from the U.S. Department of Justice Antitrust Division, asking me to appear before a Grand Jury investigating "possible criminal violations of Federal antitrust laws and related offenses and particularly price fixing in ocean transportation in the United States/European trade." The letter advised that I had the right to remain silent, to consult with a lawyer, that

anything I said might be used against me, and that nothing in the letter should be construed as an offer of immunity.

Seatrain arranged for me to consult with a lawyer, and consult I did over the next year. I don't recall what actually occurred during my appearance before the Grand Jury, but I was shocked to be advised in June, 1979, that I, along with twelve other senior executives in the industry had been indicted as were the five shipping lines at which we were each employed during the period in question.

Ocean Rate-Fixing Indictments Made

Alleged Conspiracy On US-Europe Routes

By HELEN ERICSON
Journal of Commerce Staff

WASHINGTON — A federal grand jury here has indicted five shipping lines and 13 individuals for conspiring to fix ocean freight charges between the U.S. and Europe during the early 1970s.

The shipping firms charged — on felony counts — are: Atlantic Container Line, Ltd.; American Export Lines, Inc.; Dart Containerline Company Ltd.; Hapag-Lloyd Aktiengesellschaft; Sea-Land Service, Inc.; Seatrain Lines, Inc.; and United States Lines, Inc.

The individuals — charged with a misdemeanor — are:

— Donald G. Aldridge, former executive vice president of United States Lines Inc.

— Philip E. Bates, chairman of Atlantic Container Line Services Ltd.

— Wolfgang Bohle, head of North American services for Hapag-Lloyd Aktiengesellschaft.

— Manuel Diaz, former executive director of the Associated North Atlantic Freight Conferences.

— Daniel du Bois, former chief executive officer of Dart Containerline Co. Ltd.

— Davis B. Hall, former deputy chief executive officer of Dart Containerline Co. Ltd.

— Edward J. Heine Jr., former president of United States Lines Inc.

— Arne G.M. Koch, former managing director of Atlantic Container Line Ltd.

— Howard A. Levy, an attorney employed by several ocean shipping conferences.

— J. Scott Morrison, former senior vice president, marketing, Sea-Land Service Inc.

— Arthur C. Novacek, former president and executive vice president, Container Division of Seatrain Lines Inc.

— Paul F. Richardson, former president of Sea-Land Service Inc.

— Karl-Heinz Sager, member of the board of directors and chief executive of North Atlantic services of Hapag-Lloyd Aktiengesellschaft.

There have been several reports that there have been negotiations between the indicted and the Justice Department to enter nolo contendere pleas on the charges. A Justice department spokesman, when asked about the negotiations, replied: "no comment." However, one executive in one of the shipping companies involved said that no contest pleas are tentatively agreed for fines of $450,000 on the corporate charges and $50,000 on the individual counts.

The maximum penalty under the Sherman Act is a fine of $1 million for each corporation. The penalty for the individuals charged with a misdemeanor is one year in prison and a fine of $50,000 for each person.

The indictment covers activity starting in 1971 and continuing into 1975. The companies were the seven major container lines in the U.S. European trade at that time. In 1974, the total revenue in this trade was about $1 billion, according to the Justice Department. The defendant firms are believed to have accounted for almost

(Continued on Page 31)

Rate-Fixing Indictments Handed Down

(Continued from Page 1)

90 percent of that trade, the agency adds.

John H. Shenefield, the Justice Department's assistant attorney general, Antitrust Division, said the indictments allege that the defendants agreed to fix prices outside the scope of Federal Maritime Commission approved agreements.

The agency points out that it is not illegal for ocean shippers to fix rates provided the joint activity has FMC approval. The indictment charges that the defendants did not inform the FMC of their activities.

With different lawyers representing each of the lines and the individuals involved, marathon sessions were held with the Antitrust Division, and an agreement was hammered out and announced on June 11, 1979. As a consequence of the agreement, I was to appear in court and plead *nolo contendere* (no contest) to the charges.

The Federal Courthouse in Newark, NJ, is a gloomy, gray structure, and seemed more so the day I was to appear before the U.S District Court Judge. Jeanette and I sat together on a bench outside the courtroom. I remember the shiny marble floor at which I stared gloomily during our lengthy wait. The other defendants were there as well, but aside from acknowledging one another, there was no conversation. All of us had gone through a long period of uncertainty and deep concern about our futures. The essence of the government's case was that in the course of all the various conference meetings, rate-making decisions were made between steamship conferences. Without an agreement covering such action, filed with and approved by the Federal Maritime Commission, such actions are illegal.

Finally, we were herded into the courtroom and lined up before the judge, like common criminals, as she advised that each of us was fined $50,000. This followed our earlier no-contest pleadings. Seatrain paid my fine, and I put this terrible experience behind me. None of the individuals fined suffered any professional setback as a result of this proceeding; and in fact we received a good deal of sympathy within our industry, generally being seen as the victims of a zealous Justice Department pursuing a case that would not have raised an eyebrow anywhere in Europe.

Thinking back to February 1976, I realized that my final months at Seatrain had become unbearable. I watched the company's decline, the organization falling apart and losing shipper support, profits plummeting, all of which affected me adversely. I was drinking too much, putting on weight, and never looked forward to going to the office as I had before. A change in my life was long overdue, and when the opportunity did come, it was in an incredible form, the subject of the next chapter.

*   *   *   *

Chapter 8

COLD WAR AGENT

It was a morning in June of 1976 when I received the call. "Hello, Mr. Novacek, this is Agent Foley of the FBI. Do you suppose you could join me for a cup of coffee? How about the Ramada, across from your building? There are a few things I'd like to talk to you about." This was only the second week in my new job, and I was stunned by the call. It was hard to believe that the FBI might be taking an interest in my new venture. (I have not used the agent's actual name in this account.) I heard myself say, "OK, be there in a few minutes." I hurried from my office, past my secretary, down the aisle between neat rows of matching desks, through the glass-enclosed waiting room, and onto the elevator. The office building was one of several springing up on the fringes of the colonial town of Westfield, New Jersey.

The Westfield Ramada was also new, like our company, our office building, and even our employees. I crossed the lobby into the coffee shop and found the booth in the corner of the dimly-lighted room. It was almost 11 a.m. and, this late in the morning, we were the only customers. I studied Agent Foley. Dark suit, white shirt, and striped tie, he reminded me of an aggressive bull terrier under restraint. He didn't bother to stand, but, as I sat down, he displayed his FBI credentials to me. There was no small talk. "Mr. Novacek, all we want you to do is keep us informed of the movements of your Soviet contacts visiting the United States. That shouldn't be a problem for you, should it?" I was stunned. My knowledge of the FBI was limited to television and novels. Were they recruiting me as an informant?

"Well, sir," I finally replied, "My company is just a business. We were set up to provide agency services to Soviet Steamship lines calling at American ports. Seems to me that's legal. I don't see how I can help you." His stare said, "Who the hell do you think you are?" Finally, he stood and handed me his card, saying, "I'd suggest you give it some serious thought." Crossing the street, I found my shoulders slumping as I slowly walked back to my office.

Six weeks before my encounter with the FBI, I was sitting in my office on the New Jersey waterfront, staring morosely out of my large picture window at the skyline of lower Manhattan, a very disgruntled senior executive of a large steamship company, wondering how I could extricate myself from a job which had me at odds with the company owners. The phone must have rung a half dozen times before I reluctantly answered. At first, I didn't recognize the voice with the uncommon accent. "Art, this is Valeri, could you make lunch this Friday?" Valeri Novikov was the main contact between the Soviet steamship lines and their counterparts in the United States. He attended most of the industry meetings of any significance to the newly-emerging steamship services of the Soviet Union.

At these meetings I had established a good relationship with Valeri. He was an assistant to George Maslov, head of Sovinflot, the Soviet entity responsible for establishing and coordinating the activities of all Soviet steamship agents around the globe. While Valeri was knowledgeable about international shipping matters, he could be tedious in his business dealings. He wore eyeglasses with thick lenses, and even then had to hold the written page close, occasionally removing his glasses to rub his pale blue eyes. He spoke with a slight Russian accent and in a deliberate manner, as if trying to intimidate the listener.

At our Friday lunch, Valeri introduced me to George Maslov and two other Soviets. We were in a private room at a Japanese restaurant in Midtown Manhattan. There were no chairs. While we tried to sit yoga style, not a tradition in Russia, and difficult for me with my long legs, but ended up sprawled on the floor like wounded on a battlefield. Maslov spoke English without a trace of a Russian accent, and could pass for an American anywhere in our country. Half a head shorter than my six-foot two, olive-skinned, he looked more Greek than Russian. He was well-versed in American history, cinema, sports, and other elements of our culture, and claimed he was Brooklyn-born and had spent his early years in the United States. "We're looking for someone to run an American-based company that would serve as agents for one of our steamship lines about to expand its services in the Pacific," he said. There had been rumors of these developments and I wasn't surprised by the offer. And God knows I was thoroughly depressed with my job at Seatrain, but still, the thought of working for the Soviets filled me with apprehension.

Maslov waited patiently as I struggled with a response. I should have asked for more time, but, looking back, I realize I wanted another challenge, regardless of the uncertainties. Finally I ventured, "Yes, I would be interested, but I need a better idea of what would be expected." After several hours of discussion, we agreed to meet the next day at the Lexington, a second-rate hotel used by visiting Soviets, where, around a worn table in a large, sparsely-furnished suite, we negotiated an employment agreement and a steamship agency contract. "Morflot America Shipping, Inc." came to life, owned by Sovinflot and incorporated in the United States, and soon to provide steamship agency services to Soviet vessel operators. I was named president of the new company. MORAM, as we always styled it, established offices in Clark, NJ, forty-five minutes from Sovinflot in Midtown Manhattan and five minutes from my home. We moved quickly to organize a steamship agency operation, recruiting headquarters staff, and setting up branch offices.

In 1972, there were only eight Soviet conventional cargo freighters operating on U.S. trade routes. By the time we started our agency company in 1976, 59 Soviet liner vessels, most of them newly built and designed specifically for the movement of containers, were operating between 20 U.S. ports and 30 foreign ports. Once, when I mentioned to Maslov that I was impressed with the number of new vessels joining the Soviet commercial fleet, he departed from his usual reticence in discussing political matters. "My government never wants to be in the position it was in during the Cuban missile crisis when we had only an aging merchant fleet to supply Cuba."

Three weeks after my first encounter with Agent Foley I received disturbing information from Benny, our landlord in Clark. Benny was a retired New York City police detective who had done well in real estate development. He also continued to maintain close relations with the law-enforcement community, and we had become good friends. Benny burst into my office that morning, drew up my one extra chair and sank slowly into it, befitting his considerable bulk, and without even a "hello" said, "Wanted you to know that your phone system is bugged. It was done while being installed. Keep it between us. Don't let it bother you. Not unusual for these crazy times. The Feds see a Russian behind every tree." After giving this latest development some thought, I decided there was not much I could do about it. After all, we were what we said we were, a steamship agency, and not a cover for something sinister.

Arguing different points of view: Don Aldridge and Art
(Source: TRAFFIC WORLD magazine, Dec. 6, 1976)

In addition to problems with the FBI, many of my friends in the maritime industry made no secret of their disenchantment with me for joining the "enemy." Take my friend Don Aldridge, executive vice president of United States Lines. During a brief phone call, he let me have it: "Goddamn it Art! Why would you want to work for those guys?" I knew that my new venture was strictly commercial, but I was still glad that our office was far enough from our major competitors in and around New York City to make contact with my network of business friends a rarity.

Animosity against the Soviets was also harbored by American union labor. At an industry luncheon a few months after we set up MORAM, the President of the International

Longshoremens Association, the union whose members load and unload cargoes in U.S. ports, vehemently stated, "The only thing the damn Russians have going for them is Novacek." This was not meant to be a compliment, of course, and it was followed by some hisses from the audience. The crowning touch came when the event concluded. As I was descending on a crowded escalator, one of the men in front of me whom I knew to be a manager with the Chilean Line, said to a friend, "Novacek has cost our company a lot of money with his lower rates. Some American he is."

Even my father, back in my hometown of Omaha and himself an immigrant from Czechoslovakia, asked, "Why did you have to accept the invitation to speak?" He was referring to some remarks I had made before a convention of farmers in Lincoln, suggesting ways they could sell more wheat to Russia. The headline appearing the next morning in the *Midland Business Journal* read "Native Omahan Heads Soviet Shipping Fleet," an obvious exaggeration of my position, but the damage was done. I later received several phone calls from childhood friends who had been led to believe that I was more than just a steamship agent.

Such issues aside, I must admit that I enjoyed the challenge of building a new company. As a steamship line agent, MORAM was responsible for the provision of the services required by a large cargo vessel, such as harbor pilots, tugboats, line handlers and stevedores, at all U.S. ports of call. In addition to these traditional duties, the major focus of this new company was to provide marketing, sales, pricing, customer service and equipment control for the wave of new, modern Soviet containerships being introduced to the American trades. Cargoes were stowed in large metal containers, similar to highway trailer truck bodies, stacked in neat slots that rose from the bottom of the ships' holds and reached up as many as four layers above the main deck. Sophisticated computer container-tracking programs were required to control the movements of thousands of container units.

*   *   *   *

The difficulty some Soviets had in comprehending the differences between our capitalist system and that of their communist state was illustrated by my occasional exchanges with Captain Timofiev, a former ship's captain, blustering and in-your-face, whom I chose to avoid even though he was attached to the Sovinflot office in New York. He was one of several Sovinflot representatives in the New York office who kept tabs on our progress. I believed that if I were to follow his wishes, the new venture would have extreme difficulty in succeeding, but thankfully he had no direct authority over me. "Why do you have so many people on your payroll?" he asked on one of his rare visits to our office, located as it was on the outer rim of his authorized travel zone, a radius of 35 miles from Columbus Circle in Manhattan, as mandated by the U.S. Government. With a fixed smile revealing two gold teeth, he went on, "You could start right here. I see so many people. What could they possibly be doing?" Timofiev had no idea of the staffing needs of an agency representing a large steamship company in a capitalist business environment. "Back home, we handle all these details with a few people." He didn't bother to mention that in Moscow a handful of government bureaus, in typical communist fashion, arranged all exports and imports. Exasperated, I responded, "Well, this isn't back home. We have thousands of different companies importing and exporting, and must service them all."

Not long after that, Sovinflot recalled Timofiev from New York. One evening several years later, while walking through my hotel lobby in Moscow, I was enveloped in a Russian bear hug and kissed on both cheeks, as alcoholic fumes encircled my head. I recognized my old critic, Captain Timofiev. "Artur, my dear old friend, it's been so long. How are you?" It seems Sovinflot had posted him to Murmansk. Leaving Moscow in a few days, he was having a farewell celebration. Murmansk was one of the northernmost ports in the Soviet Union, celebrated as the port of entry for American military aid during World War II. Isolated and cold, with long dark winters, Murmansk could hardly be considered a desirable location. I wished him good luck.

Liev Kourdryatsev, who was my business counterpart in Canada, was quite the opposite of Timofiev. He was trained to work in the capitalist world, having received extensive business experience in Paris, attached to the French company that represented the Soviet steamship lines. He now managed the Soviet-owned steamship agency in Canada, which had few restrictions on the jobs held by Soviet citizens or the movements of Soviet representatives. A Russian version of a young Clint Eastwood, he had the same tall, slender, powerful frame, light brown hair, and a rugged, handsome face beginning to show lines of wear. Fluent in English and French, he seemed at home in Vancouver. On my first visit, Kourdryatsev and I were dining at one the city's best seafood restaurants when he remarked, "Novacek, I could see that you were impressed when you got a look at our setup today. I'll bet you didn't think we could do it." And, of course, he was right. In addition to his business acumen, he had learned to enjoy the benefits of our western society that included living in a large apartment and driving a new American car.

Kourdryatsev had some strongly biased opinions that I attributed to his early training under the Communist system. I recall an occasion when we were together in New York Harbor, in the spacious Captain's Cabin aboard the Soviet passenger ship *Odessa*, eating caviar canapés and drinking vodka before lunch. For some reason unknown to me, the Captain expressed concern that his ship might be sabotaged. Kourdryatsev commented, "I wouldn't put it past those Jew bastards. You should face up to it Novacek, your country is run by the Jews." I'm sure my face registered dismay, but it was the Captain who spoke up, saying firmly," I don't want to hear that kind of talk on my ship." Perhaps it was such lapses in his usual controlled conduct that led to Kourdryatsev being recalled to Moscow four months later to join the staff of Sovinflot.

Kourdryatsev's replacement in Vancouver, Anatoly Koukshenko, was a charming, friendly, former master of a Soviet supertanker. In his mid-thirties, he was tall, dark-haired, and moved with the grace of a skilled seafarer. He was probably chosen to replace Kourdryatsev because of his personable traits. Unfortunately, he had great difficulty bridging the cultural gap. I remember the first time I visited him in Vancouver when he confided, "Art, I'm exhausted. My apartment has a balcony overlooking this beautiful city. I spend most of my nights there alone in a reclining chair. I can't get used to being here." I tried to understand his feelings, assuring him that in a short time he should be acclimated to his new surroundings. But with no comparable experience of my own, I was mistaken. An insight into what may well have been Anatoly's feelings is provided by David K. Shipler, Moscow correspondent for the *New York Times* from 1977 to 1979, the same period as my association with the Russians. In his memoirs, "RUSSIA: Broken Idols, Solemn Dreams," he writes:

> *In all respects the United States looks chaotic to many Russians. Politically because of its pluralism, it seems disorderly, directionless, frighteningly disharmonious. Economically, because of its diversity and decentralization, life seems insecure, uncertain, dangerously unpredictable. Socially, the country seems riven by street crime and racial conflict. It makes for a terrifying spectacle. Russians' propaganda plays to their natural affinity for order, planning, and authority, magnifying the discord in American life.*

*   *   *

It was a relief to escape the criticisms of my competitors and the interference of my local Soviet advisors by visiting my new principals overseas. En route to our first meeting with the Far East Shipping Company (FESCO), headquartered in Vladivostok, our executive vice president, Bill Heffernan, and I boarded the Soviet passenger ship *Baikal* in Yokohama for the last leg of our journey to Nakhodka, a port in Far Eastern Russia, a two-hour drive from Vladivostok. Because westerners were barred from visiting Vladivostok, site of a major Soviet naval base, the Russians drove to Nakhodka for our meetings.

The four-day voyage from Yokohama to Nakhodka allowed us ample time to prepare for the meeting with our principals at FESCO. With the Captain's approval, we set up shop in a large stateroom located midships, with the luxury of a long conference table. A chicken bone on the worn rug pretty well summed up the condition of the entire ship. The *Baikal* was one of two passenger ships providing regular service between Nakhodka and Yokohama. About 30 years old, it had a capacity of 300 passengers, staterooms with two bunks each and adjoining bathrooms, and uncovered steel bulkheads throughout, no effort having been made to cover them with any kind of paneling.

A voice shouted from the wharf, "Welcome to Nakhodka!" It was my friend, Valeri Novikov, who had traveled more than 2,000 miles from Moscow to introduce us to the

Welcoming party at Nakhodka: Valeri Novikov (second from left), Sasha Buriy (second from right, back row)

FESCO staff. His small group wove its way through the departing and embarking passengers, many of whom were connecting with the Siberian Express trains linking Vladivostok and Nakhodka with Moscow. Novikov introduced us to a half dozen FESCO managers, one of whom stands out in my memory. Alexsander ("Sasha") Buriy and I connected immediately. In time, I grew to consider him as close a friend as any of my business acquaintances in the United States. General Manager of the liner department of FESCO, he was in his mid-thirties, broad shouldered and muscular, with unruly brown hair and a broad smile. He beamed, "We're planning a dinner on board in your honor tonight, hosted by the president of our company." Buriy was from the Ukraine, then a part of the Soviet Union, but I didn't perceive a distinction between him and the Russian managers. Perhaps I should have, since the Ukraine was one of the first of the republics to withdraw when the Soviet Union disintegrated. But I did wonder why there seemed to be such a competitive edge between Buriy and the others.

In my relations with the Soviets we avoided conversations of a personal nature. I was surprised one day when Buriy commented on the hard life he had had as a youth on a collective farm. "I drove a tractor when I was sixteen, and looked forward to getting off that farm as soon as I could. Pursuing a career in shipping seemed as good a way as any." The Ukraine was the Soviet Union's breadbasket, with huge expanses of land devoted to growing various types of grain. Being from Nebraska and having worked on my uncles' farms in the summer months, I could relate to Sasha's desire to escape that grind.

Inspecting Port of Nakhodka: Sasha Buriy (foreground), Art (on right)

Prior to our visit to Nakhodka, I was not aware that FESCO operated a fleet of more than three hundred vessels of all types, managed all Soviet Far Eastern ports, and was an auxiliary of the Soviet Navy. Valentin Biankin, the President of FESCO, held the rank of Admiral, though he rarely wore his uniform. He was a highly-decorated veteran of World War II, and a recipient of the Order of the Soviet Union, the country's highest honor. At dinner, I was seated at the Captain's table in the main dining room of the *Baikal*, surrounded by about a hundred FESCO staff, all of us waiting for the main attraction. We were not disappointed. Admiral Biankin swept into the room with his entourage.

Charismatic and exotic looking, he reminded me of Yul Brynner in the "The King and I," only somewhat heavier and with more hair on his head. He affected not to speak English and used Valeri as his translator. It's interesting to note that Yul Brynner's roots were in this part of Russia, and, in fact, his family was the original owner of FESCO before the Russian Revolution. After a few shots of vodka, I even began to feel that I was dealing with Yul Brynner, and that the President of FESCO was really the King of Siam.

The rest of that evening was a blur, with all of us enjoying the bliss of endless bottles of vodka, fueling one toast after another. It was more than a blur for Bill Heffernan, who took up the challenge of matching Yul glass for glass until his head plunked down on his dinner plate, and he had to be carried off to his stateroom. Bill was slender and sandy-haired, 41 years old, with a low boiling point and a reddened face to go with it. He also thought he could handle his liquor. Perhaps that notion changed the next day.

On board the BAIKAL: Art, in background, with FESCO managers-teaching the essentials of marketing

The *Baikal* was held in port as the venue for our meetings, a strange way to use an asset, and the FESCO and Sovinflot groups stayed on board, typifying the Communist system at work in Russia. The concept of commercial competition and profit-making was relatively new. I was there to teach these young managers the tools of capitalism, and how to play that game. They had been trained in a system of non-competition in business, and one company, FESCO, controlled all maritime activities in their region, but they were well-educated and proved to be good students.

The main subject was, of course, marketing. FESCO had no marketing plan. It was relatively easy to make them the beneficiaries of both my MBA in marketing and the real life experience I had in developing similar plans for earlier businesses: namely, in the case of FESCO, to identify the volume of cargoes moving in FESCO's trade lanes, to calculate the number of container slots which needed to be filled on FESCO's container ships to produce a profit, to develop lists of potential customers actively shipping over those trade lanes, and to formalize a sales program to secure the cargoes necessary to achieve the volume and revenue goals established. The fact that I was in possession of much of the requisite data, retained from my time at Seatrain Line, was crucial to our plan. The presentations were well received, and I believe we accomplished our mission. For the first time, a major Soviet steamship line was ready to take on its formidable Western competitors. In the isolated atmosphere of the Soviet Far East, I had no qualms about my contributions to our Cold War rival. Yet such feelings would emerge later, like a cancer that had been in remission.

Departure day finally came. We stood at the rail on the main deck, shouting goodbyes to our Soviet colleagues on the dock. Rolls of paper streamers of various colors fluttered between ship and shore. I noticed a long black limousine as it parked close to the raised gangway, and was surprised to see the president of FESCO join the ranks of well-wishers. I threw a streamer in his general direction and somehow it floated down perfectly within his reach. He seized the end, and we were briefly joined together. As our eyes locked, it seemed that Yul Brynner and I were the only ones present, and I imagined that I was Marco Polo visiting the court of Kublai Khan, not just a steamship company agent calling on his principals. It was a novel way to escape the realities of the Cold War.

*   *   *   *

Back home again, I wasn't ready for the blow that came. I was having breakfast at my house when the phone rang. It was Bill Heffernan. "You'd better get over here. We've got a problem." As I quickly headed for MORAM headquarters, I could never have guessed the extent of the problem. Hurrying onto the elevator, I went up the three floors to our offices. Before the elevator stopped, I knew there was trouble. The doors opened and I stepped into an eye-stinging fog of gray smoke and a foul smell not unlike burning plastic. In a state of shock, I spotted Bill talking to several uniformed firemen. As I approached, he exclaimed, "Somebody sabotaged our computer facility. It happened sometime last night, and I got a call about an hour ago from our landlord. We haven't been able to determine how it happened. Not only is our computer system wiped out, but our offices are unusable. The desks, furniture, all are covered with black soot. I've already talked to Benny [our landlord], and we're checking for temporary space to resume some of the operations." We were in our fifth month, and our new, state-of-the-art Hewlett-Packard computer and all the accompanying software was destroyed. In those days, mainframe hardware was expensive and impressive. Our computer programs had been recently developed to serve sophisticated equipment-control needs, tracking some 5,000 pieces of equipment as well as maintaining our financial accounting and records as we evolved into a full-scale agency operation.

I was devastated, and could think of nothing better to do than hurriedly walk back to the elevator, make the slow descent, walk out the building entrance, climb into my car, and begin driving aimlessly around the area. The questions whirled in my head. What do we do now? How do we keep running? What do I tell our principals? How do we deal with our staff? What do we tell our customers? After calming down a bit, I knew I had to go back and face reality. This time, Bill greeted me with "I think we have things under control. Benny is allowing us to shift most of our things to an unused space next to ours. We've already cleaned some desks and moved them over. The phone company is working with us to provide extensions to the new area. We've checked, and our insurance covers us. I've also been in touch with Hewlett-Packard arranging replacement equipment on an emergency basis." Bill had done everything that needed to be done.

Even though the fire was investigated by the local authorities, we were never able to determine if the blaze was the result of equipment failure or an act of arson. I suppose I was being irrational when I tried to connect it to our government, but I realize that I could hardly blame the FBI, who hadn't surfaced since our early encounter. Needless to say, my principals, the Soviets, were none too well-regarded by almost anyone in the United States, so I surmised that somehow this unfortunate event came with the territory.

*   *   *   *

FORTUNE magazine had it right in their February 1977 article about profit-minded corporations set up by the Soviet Union in the West, which featured MORAM. The sidebar special which carried my picture was headlined, "When Your Home Office Is Moscow." One of those trips to my "home office" brought Cold War realities to light in a different but telling fashion. While I had met with our Sovinflot principals in Moscow earlier that first year, it was the visit I made in December that stayed with me. It was snowing outside as I peered through my window in the venerable National Hotel that faces the Kremlin and Red Square. It was about 3 a.m., and I couldn't sleep, having flown in just a few hours earlier. Red Square and the streets around it were covered with a thick blanket of snow. Light came only from street lamps dimmed by falling snowflakes, creating eerie reflections of the dark shadows cast by a handful of Muscovites shuffling through the deepening snow. "Am I really here again?" I mused. The Kremlin, in particular, drew my attention. It looked more sinister than usual. Lights flickered in some of the windows. I wondered what our cold war protagonists might be up to. My short visits to Moscow seemed only to magnify the inherent mystery of the city and its inhabitants.

Some sense of the cultural shock that faced visiting Russians in the U.S. was with me that morning as I set off on my ten-block walk to the Sovinflot offices. It was cold. My hands were stiff, even in fleece-lined gloves and thrust deeply into my coat pockets. I was wearing my Russian mink-fur hat with the flaps down over my icy ears and a heavy gray

143

woolen topcoat. The Russians around me, heading to their offices, wore dark overcoats, mostly black, and hats like mine. I thought I was a fast walker, but they flowed around me like a stream past a boulder. No one spoke.

My route took me by the statue of Feliks Dzerzhinsky, the first head of the infamous KGB, standing tall in the square fronting KGB headquarters and Lubyanka prison. I'd heard about the cells in the basements of that building where torture and death of dissidents was routinely carried out. A melodrama began to unfold in my mind. Here I was, representing a branch of the "evil empire," in the words of Ronald Reagan. I made a conscious effort to erase those thoughts. "Come on Art, you're only a shipping agent providing commercial services to a customer." However, I knew that the better I performed those services, the more competitive the Soviets would become in their efforts to seize a share of the rapidly growing world trade.

Arriving at my destination, I found an elderly World War II veteran, the front of his worn jacket festooned with ribbons and medals, who opened the heavy wooden door for me. It was not uncommon to see such a proud display on both men and women throughout the Soviet Union. I was ushered into a large conference room with a long dark table set with bottles of water and drinking glasses and side cabinets sporting fake mahogany veneers. After a short wait, the local delegation entered, one after the other, outnumbering me six to one. These meetings were more like negotiations, no matter what the subject, even though I was their commercial agent, and we were supposedly on the same side in our business activities. Valeri Novikov, squinting at me through his thick glasses, began with, "Good to see you Novacek. What are you trying to get out of us today?" Friend or not, Valeri echoed the tone of all our meetings.

I stayed in a number of hotels in Russia, several recently built. Even in these new hotels, some things never seemed to change: poor service, worn outfits, pervasive body odor, and deplorable English. The services reflected the lack of competition between hotels and a lack of training in customer service. Employees working at the new hotels were clones of those found at much older ones. Perhaps the most interesting people on staff were the big Slavic-featured women who were the keepers of order on each floor, ensconced at worn wooden desks close to the elevator doors. I winced at the pressure applied to my arm as I tried to board the elevator. I didn't understand Russian, but could swear she cried, "Give me the goddamned key." Returning to my room each day, it was these charming ladies who muttered, (I believe), "OK you can have it back now, you stupid foreigner."

Once, strolling through the corridor to my room, I glanced into a small room, door ajar, and saw a bank of tape recorders with big reels slowly turning. Did this mean the rumor was true, that the phones in the hotel were bugged? It was easy to develop paranoia in this country where every third person looked to me as if he might be KGB. But perhaps the reason people I passed sometimes stared at me so intently was that they hadn't seen many Americans, and my fur hat wasn't enough of a disguise. Regardless, I made a point not to use my hotel phone after that.

An official written invitation was required to visit the Soviet Union. While there, a government bureau, "Intourist," handled all hotel assignments. After disembarking and clearing immigration and customs, incoming airline passengers reported to the Intourist desk to pick up their hotel bookings, never knowing in advance to which hotel they were assigned. Then they all gathered for long periods outside the terminal, waiting for Intourist buses to take them to their hotels, where they reported to the Intourist check-in counter to get their room assignments.

I remember one time arriving during a heavy snowstorm. After I picked up my hotel assignment, instead of milling around with the rest of the crowd, I dashed out into the heavy falling snow, quickly located an empty bus, pounded on its door and was grudgingly allowed to board by a driver hunched over the steering wheel with only his eyes showing through his turned up coat collar and scarf. "Take me to the Intourist Hotel," I gasped. "Intourist?" he responded. I vigorously nodded my head, up and down, and off we went, just the driver and me, leaving a gaggle of other passengers struggling through the deep snow. "Wow" I thought, "I finally beat the system." It was an exhilarating ride to the hotel, barreling through snow as deep as our tires, no other vehicle in sight.

Departing from Moscow could be intimidating. Immigration officers wore uniforms and hats reminiscent of the ones worn by the Gestapo, or so it seemed to me, as they stared, unsmiling, through the glass windows of their cubbyholes, first at my face and then at my passport as I was cleared for departure. Climbing the ramp to the plane, and hearing "Welcome on board" from a pretty Pan American stewardess, I finally relaxed, "almost like home," and settled down to a vodka martini.

In these post-Soviet times it is difficult to conjure up the atmosphere within the Soviet Union during the Cold War years, perhaps best summed up by Pulitzer Prize-winning journalist David Shipler:

> *Military secrecy is so broadly defined that Westerners need to develop a whole new set of instincts when they get to the Soviet Union. Officials and much of the population proceed as if they were in the midst of a conventional war, one predating the high technology of reconnaissance satellites and intercontinental nuclear tipped missiles. No pictures may be taken of bridges, ports, railway junctions, men in uniform, police stations, or military installations, except with special permission. No photography whatever is allowed from airliners, as if the Pentagon's satellites were not repeatedly recording every visible detail of Soviet territory.*

*   *   *   *

Chapter 9

COLD WAR AGENT ROUND TWO

Two other Soviet managers, one Russian and the other Ukrainian, are important to this story. The first, a veteran of World War II, worked for the Baltic Steamship Company (Baltic) at its headquarters in Leningrad. When MORAM was named agents for Baltic's Great Lakes Service as well as a newly established service to the Middle East, Bill Heffernan and I were invited to visit Leningrad, where we met the most mysterious of our Soviet contacts, Captain Ivan Gonchorov, manager of Baltic's North American Services.

In the spring of 1977, we journeyed by train from Moscow, arriving at dawn in a city built literally stone-by-stone under the direction of Czar Peter the Great some 300 years earlier. Off we went by taxi to the Baltic offices in the sprawling port complex. "Come in, come in!" We heard this invitation spoken in a deep, graveled voice as we sat nervously in the tiny reception area. "Looks like I don't have any choice but to use your agency. Orders from Moscow. What do you think you can do for me?" So this was the famous Gonchorov, reportedly a colonel in the KGB, rumored to have slipped into the United States through Canada on a number of occasions. His mystique was probably enhanced by his appearance: barrel-chested, thick, strong arms, a wide face with furrowed eyebrows and a crooked smile, an image not unlike American actor Ernest Borgnine.

Baltic was another of the Soviet Union's giant shipping groups. With a fleet of more than 250 vessels, Baltic also controlled all maritime activities in the port of Leningrad. Gonchorov arranged for us to view most of these operations, a grueling tour that exhausted us, much to his delight. We stayed three days in a vintage hotel, directly across from the *Aurora*, the Russian cruiser which in October, 1917, had fired the shot that signaled rebellious soldiers, sailors, and workers to storm the Winter Palace and then the residence of the Provisional Government, changing Russian history forever. The ship is now a museum. In the days that followed, I enjoyed my early morning runs past the enormous statue of Peter the Great on his charger, its front hooves slashing the air, supported by only one of its hind legs, a unique posture for a statue that large. It was in a square close to the Soviet Naval Academy, and, as I passed naval cadets forming for their morning routines, I wondered if any of them would ever be manning Soviet submarines that might face off against our own.

Gonchorov did not offer to dine with us that first evening, so we were left to our own devices. As we finished our dinner in the crowded hotel restaurant, a Russian dance band began to play. Bill and I were part way through a bottle of vodka, relaxing as we listened to the music. We heard a voice behind us. "Mind if I join you?" His English was good, with only a faint Russian accent. A pleasant-looking young man, he was well dressed in a pin-striped gray suit and solid-colored tie, and would have looked at home on London's Bond Street. "Of course," I said, wondering why he should pick our table. We exchanged business cards and he sat down. "Have you gentlemen been enjoying your stay in Leningrad?" After I mumbled an affirmative response, he attempted to lighten things up with some small talk about the sights in Leningrad, saying that his work was promoting tourism.

Finally he asked, "And with whom have you been visiting?" We recounted our day at the Baltic Steamship Company and in particular our visit with Captain Gonchorov. "And did you find him cooperative?" "Yes, we are well along in completing our business." "Which is what?" By that time, Bill and I had grown a little nervous, and the conversation continued in the same vein. We were relieved when he finally departed after helping us finish our vodka. The next morning at breakfast we were sitting with several English businessmen, one of whom said, "I saw you chaps in the restaurant last night. Do you know who that Russian was who joined you?" "No," I admitted. He went on, "We understand he's KGB." Once again I was reminded that there was a dark side to the world in which my Soviet business colleagues worked.

The last of the three major Soviet maritime combines was the Black Sea Shipping Company (Blasco), based in Odessa, a port on the Black Sea and the largest city in the Ukraine. Eugene Tchecka was the Managing Director of Blasco Lines. In his early forties, he had a cheerful disposition and an athletic physique that he worked hard to maintain. He took pride in his exercise routine which consisted of a short jog from his apartment in Odessa and a swim at dawn in the Black Sea. Serious about his business, he constantly asked questions about all aspects of shipping in the United States.

I visited Odessa several times, taking commuter flights from Moscow, and was a curiosity to my fellow passengers, just as Russians were at that time when flying the "friendly skies" in the U.S. The Russian aircraft were old, with cramped seating and the smell of cleaning fluids mixed with body odor permeating the cabin. The flights were generally late and were considered risky by many Westerners. There was a plane crash somewhere in the Soviet Union every other week or so, which for the most part went unreported in the global press.

Odessa, while situated on the banks of the Black Sea seemed in many respects a Mediterranean city. Most of its citizens were not of pure Slavic stock, but mixtures going back to ancient Greek settlements, Phoenician traders, and even Tartar and Turkish conquerors. They were friendly and outgoing, and made business almost secondary to socializing, including evenings at the famous Odessa opera house. Opera was not a pastime high on my list, but somehow it was made more enjoyable by attending with the enthusiastic crowds assembled there. My most memorable event in Odessa was a luncheon given in my honor by the captain of one of the new Blasco ships. After a couple of hours sampling four or five courses and going through ample vodka, Ukrainian wine, and brandy, I was feeling no pain as I gallantly turned to the captain's lovely wife, or so she seemed by then, and out of my mouth came, "Could I have the pleasure of a dance, with the captain's permission of course?"

Although the captain's record player had been softly playing some delightful Russian folk songs, no one was dancing. My last reasonably clear recollection was that I did indeed dance with that genteel lady in the confined stateroom. Things were certainly not clear to me as I was assisted down the gangway while mumbling my thanks for the generous hospitality and gently lowered into my seat in the awaiting van. Consciousness returned when I awoke three hours later in my bed at the hotel, with a splitting headache. My stock seemed to go up with my friends in the Blasco office for having so clearly displayed my liking for true Ukrainian hospitality.

My relationship with Eugene Tchecka remained very close. In the summer of 1979 he invited Jeanette and me to take a cruise on the new Blasco cruise ship, the *Kazakhstan*. After spending several days in Moscow, we flew to Odessa, where Tchecka met us at the airport, presented a bouquet of flowers, and took us directly to the ship. Eugene's attractive wife, Valeria, was able to join us on the cruise. She had never socialized with Americans before, and in fact she was the only wife of any of my Soviet contacts I ever met, aside, of course, from the captain's wife, my dancing partner aboard ship. One of the principal reasons for this lack of family contact with my colleagues may have been their embarrassment regarding their cramped and sparsely furnished apartments.

The Kazakhstan had a roll-on roll-off capability, which allowed Tchecka's car, with driver, to be driven directly onto the vessel so that it would be available to us at every port of call. "How about that, Art?" he said, as we were shown to our stateroom, the owner's suite. "This is only one of a number of passenger ships we have, many devoted to providing free cruises to outstanding workers from our factories and collective farms, not like you Americans where only the rich can cruise."

Of course, there were some differences between the service on this ship and that on cruises we had taken on Grace Line's Santa Rosa and Santa Paula. For instance, there were three seatings for meals and the passengers on each seating were expected to use and reuse the same napkins. I managed to persuade Eugene, as he had become known to us, to get us our own napkins. We bought our wine at each port stop, some from black-market operators. In Sukhumi, for example, wine was taken from vats stored in one small room. An elderly woman waited on us in the tiny, unmarked house, where she lived in the other room. We also purchased fresh vegetables and fruit in outdoor markets at every port of call. The tomatoes, onions, pears, and watermelons we bought were all grown locally, and in general were much larger than their counterparts in the U.S. The local yogurt was especially good. We took the vegetables and fruit back to the ship where the chef prepared them especially for us, and served them at dinner.

Our cruise was an extraordinary experience with calls at Novorossiysk, Batumi, Sukhumi, Sochi, and Yalta. We were the only Westerners on board and quite an anomaly. For the most part, the other passengers were ordinary Soviet citizens who, in the comfort

Jeanette and Eugene Tchecka on the beach at Yalta, 1978

of the ship, may well have thought they were in paradise. The ports of call, especially Sochi, also provided vacation facilities to hundreds of Soviets. The entire city of Sochi was declared tobacco-smoke-free, since it had a number of clinics and sanitariums treating patients with cancer and other tobacco-related diseases. I don't recall seeing anyone smoke there. Traveling with Eugene, who knew these ports well, we usually had lunch at a quaint local restaurant, with our custom being the enjoyment of two bottles of wine with the meal.

Back in the United States, things hadn't changed. The hostility of the U.S. government, which I had first encountered at my meeting with Special Agent Foley of the FBI, continued, and, in fact, increased. Congress passed the Controlled Carrier Act requiring that all freight rates charged by steamship lines under the ownership or control of their respective governments be filed 48 hours in advance of their effective date in order to allow privately-owned carriers adequate time to respond. While the bill applied to the Venezuelan Line, the Polish Ocean Line, and a few others, it was aimed primarily at the Soviets. The service frequencies provided by Soviet steamship lines were generally inferior to those of established carriers, and that, combined with pervasive anti-Soviet sentiment, resulted in lower freight rates that were necessary to induce American shippers to move their cargoes on Soviet vessels.

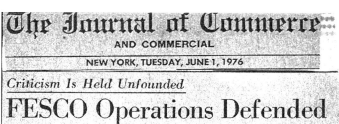

The Journal of Commerce
AND COMMERCIAL
NEW YORK, TUESDAY, JUNE 1, 1976

Criticism Is Held Unfounded
FESCO Operations Defended

By CHARLES F. DAVIS
Journal of Commerce Staff

Far East Shipping Co.'s (FESCO) operations could better serve as a model of rectitude and efficiency for other carriers instead of a target for largely unfounded criticism, according to Arthur C. Novacek.

In an address before the Maritime Associates Thursday night, Mr. Novacek, president of the Russian-flag line's U.S. general agency, Morflot America Shipping Co., said that in contrast to the activities of many other carriers, FESCO's transpacific operations are "totally clean."

His reference was obviously to the rebating and other malpractices which persist in many U.S. offshore liner trades.

"The chairman of the Federal Maritime Commission should be proud of us," Mr. Novacek said.

'Within Differential'

FESCO's five monthly sailings between the West Coast and the Far East, conducted outside rate conferences on the routes, are on a tariff basis well within the differential generally accepted between independent and conference carriers, Mr. Novacek said.

Terming reports that the Russian-flag carrier cut as much as 40 per cent off conference tariff structures as false, Mr. Novacek said

that FESCO's rates are no more than from 7 to 15 per cent under conference levels.

Defending FESCO's continued operations as an independent, Mr. Novacek held that independent carriers have a definite place in liner trades because of the "healthy" competition they provide and suggested that conferences themselves "serve as a breeding ground for malpractices."

Soviets Cost Conscious

Russian maritime officials, Mr. Novacek asserted are "definitely" cost conscious, contrary to reports that the Soviet Union's maritime activities are conducted on terms which are outside the economic considerations which govern the operations of free world shipping.

FESCO, he said recently lost a big project shipment from Southeast Asia to the West Coast as a result of the rate offered by an American-flag carrier.

Participation of FESCO's containerships on the Transpacific route has not been of a scope which threatens the existence of other carriers, Mr. Novacek said:

Cargo Share

The line's vessels account for about 2 per cent of the total containerized cargo moving in the trade and the Russian-flag carrier is the smallest of all the containership operators serving the routes, he noted.

FESCO's containerships have a capacity of about 323 20-foot boxes or the equivalent, which he described as about the size of vessels

serving in feeder operations for other carriers.

He acknowledged, however, that FESCO's Far East service, recently expanded to include a minibridge operation from the U.S. East Coast, may ultimately be assigned containerships having a capacity of 728 containers.

Mr. Novacek, in answer to a question from the floor, said he believed that Russian shipping officials would, under appropriate circumstances, make known operational costs.

The question was raised in relation to various congressional legislative proposals, including the Senate's Inouye bill, which would require third-flag carriers in U.S. foreign trade to justify their rate structures if these were notably lower than conference tariffs.

I had made myself the central spokesman and defender of the Soviet position on this critical matter, even though I had no instructions of any kind from my Soviet principals. My rationale for rising to the occasion was that I felt it essential that the Soviet shipping lines put forward a logical position to justify the inroads they were making in the marketplace, which was clearly a sensible public relations and commercial decision. (I should have charged substantial public relations fees, as Washington lobbyists do today.)

I continued to have a difficult time explaining to my friends, professional contacts, and even the many customers of Soviet lines why I was so personally involved. But I was well known in the maritime industry, and this gave creditability to the Soviet position as I presented it.

The widespread hostility to the Soviet Union and its many maritime businesses cast my mind back to my days at Grace Line. Twelve years had passed, but my memories were clear. An interesting individual who harbored his share of anti-Soviet feelings, had arrived on the scene at the time. "Mr. Novacek, my name is Felix Grab. I'm a recent immigrant from Czechoslovakia. I was a journalist in Prague, but I have sought refuge in your country to escape the oppressive communist regime in my country. Problem is, I can't find a job. I noticed your name in some newspaper articles. It sounds Czech to me, and I thought maybe you could help me." He was a short, plump man with bristly graying hair and thick eyeglasses. His mouth wore a continual smile and sprayed a fine mist of spittle every time he spoke. I sat back in my chair at the Grace Line offices and eyed him up and down, trying to figure out what to say. I felt a responsibility to try to help him, perhaps because my father was also an immigrant from Czechoslovakia. But how? He had no skills that would meet any of our needs at Grace Line.

"Well Mr. Grab, give me some time to think about it. Come back next week." Grab had gone on to tell me some of his misfortunes in Prague. It seems that in addition to his being Jewish, he was also a thoroughly anti-communist journalist, not a great combination in those days in that country. His English was good, if rather stilted, but his experience and abilities apparently were not enough to land him a position in journalism in our country.

Grace Line was then just entering the container age, building up a pool of 17-foot containers carried on deck on conventional breakbulk ships. The locations of these units were manually tracked on a magnetic board, a far cry from today's sophisticated computerized equipment-control systems. This tracking function was performed by a single clerk who worked in a glass-walled office, part of the traffic and booking section. The responsible clerk at that particular time proved inept in maintaining the rapidly growing needs of the equipment-control department and was moved to another position. Thus, a position opened up with no unusual technical requirements, so why not hire Felix Grab to do it? And so it happened that Felix took control of Grace Line's containers and chassis. Since this operation was part of the traffic department, I had overall responsibility and consequently almost daily contact with Felix, as accurate tracking of containers and chassis became more critical to our container operations.

Felix helped develop our routines for matching empty containers with container cargoes being booked, dispatching them by trucker for pick-up and delivery shipside; the assignment of various sizes and types of container; and the other myriad tasks required by this new method of cargo movement After nearly two years of this work, Felix appeared in my office one day. "Mr. Novacek", he said, "You'll never know how much I appreciate what you've done for me, but I think I've finally found a way to get back to journalism. There is no publication that specializes in the use of containers in international trade, so I'm starting one. It will be called *Container News.*" I became his first regular advertiser, placing full-page Grace Line ads in every monthly edition.

I supported Felix in other ways too, encouraging my friends in the containership industry to advertise, and even wrote some articles for his publication. We remained good friends right up to the day that he learned I was going to represent steamship lines of the Soviet Union, which he hated with a passion, both for its export of communism and for the suppression of Czechoslovakia. I'll never forget the day he called. "Art, how could you, of all people, agree to represent those bastards? Don't expect me to be friendly in future editorials in my magazine." And he wasn't. I remember one of his articles in which he referred to me as a "hired gun" for the Soviet Lines.

In time, he changed the name of his magazine to *Transport 2000* and his own name to Mark Felice. His publication was no longer devoted solely to containers but covered a broad spectrum of international shipping issues. Felix (or Mark) passed away before the disintegration of the Soviet Union, probably considering me a misguided tool of the Soviets right up to the end.

But that had been twelve years ago, and my position representing the Soviets was troubling me now. Then, quite unexpectedly, an opportunity to become president of a new Puerto Rican government-owned steamship service between the U.S. mainland and

San Juan presented itself. The possibility to make this move resulted from the close personal relationship I had developed over many years with the managing director of the new enterprise. It came at a low point in my self-esteem, and I saw that it would immediately thrust me back into the American steamship community. Once again I turned to George Maslov, the head of Sovinflot, who agreed to meet with me during his next visit to New York which was already scheduled to occur in a few weeks.

Our meeting date finally came. It was a gloomy, overcast day when Jeanette and I arrived at the Lexington Hotel. " I'm not looking forward to this," I said to her as we waited in the lobby. Finally, after an hour of rehearsing in my mind the approaches I might take, there he was. "Hello, sorry to keep you waiting, Art, why don't we go up to my room? I hope you don't mind waiting a bit longer, Jeanette." Like most Russians, Maslov was a heavy smoker, and when I recall those days I remember smoke-filled rooms. This room was no different, and the air was heavy with stale smoke. I gasped, recovered my breath, and then explained the offer I had received and why I found it so interesting. "You know, George, it's been very difficult for me lately to continue meeting the special demands I feel are necessary to represent your lines." Maslov listened quietly as he leaned back on the well-used sofa. Then he looked out the dirty window at the darkening skies. There was a long pause. Finally, he turned to me. "Well, Art, we don't want to lose you. What will it take to make you happy?" As usual, he had gotten directly to the point.

George Maslov was an enigma. A product of the Soviet Communist system, he was thoroughly comfortable doing business in the capitalist world. My friend Don Aldridge, of United States Lines, had once recounted to me a conversation he had had with Maslov while they were seat companions on a plane trip. With his blunt personality and outspokenness, Don sometimes seemed naïve. The conversation began something like this: "George, why do you want to stay in the Soviet Union? You speak perfect English and you are very familiar with the many benefits our system provides. Why not defect?" It was true that Maslov could have passed for an American, with his American accent and the features of a second-generation Greek, but he was a hard-core member of the Soviet Communist Party. Otherwise, he would never have been allowed to travel extensively and deal with foreigners all over the world. Don told me that Maslov handled what was really an awkward situation calmly and diplomatically, ignoring Don's remark.

It was this Maslov with whom I was negotiating. I thought I could achieve my goal of leaving by setting unreasonable stakes. "Well, George, for some time now I've wanted a percentage interest in the company, but I know you can't do that under your system. So instead, I might consider staying for a 50 percent increase in salary?" I was confident that this approach would provide a gracious way to end the relationship. But without hesitation he responded, "Consider it done, Art." Perhaps, subconsciously, that salary increase had been my objective all along. In any event, I ended up with an offer I couldn't refuse. This wise Russian had resolved the issue with four little words.

*   *   *   *

MORAM, as a start-up operation, was forced to recruit for every position, some 300 staff in the United States and a dozen overseas. Our Soviet principals didn't attempt to insert their own people into our organization as they did elsewhere, probably because U.S. law made this so difficult, and it was a godsend for me to have a free hand. The minimum objective set for us by Sovinflot was to cover our overhead expenses and at least break even. The overriding mission was to help make our principals, the Soviet lines, efficient and profitable. Achieving these goals depended largely on our human resources. Our main challenge was marketing FESCO's Japanese service, our major income source. I believed it essential that I recruit managers who understood Japan and related well to the Japanese.

The most successful of these new employees proved to be a former U.S. Navy nuclear submarine officer. Despite having spent four years playing tag with Soviet submarines, Steve Quaiver seemed fascinated by the prospect of working for his former adversaries and particularly to do so in a position involving U.S.-Japanese trade. While on active duty, Quaiver had enjoyed several shore leaves in Japan and was captivated by the

Japanese culture. After his discharge from the Navy, he had opted to return to Japan and continue his education at Tokyo University. Of medium height, strongly built from years of free-weight exercises, typical of submariners, he was an extrovert and the life of the party in social settings. He seemed a perfect fit for a new position created by MORAM, our representative attached to the Tokyo headquarters of FESCO's Japanese agents. His task was to ensure that priority attention be given to MORAM's marketing needs, recognizing that the Japanese agents also represented a number of other Soviet services. Quaiver quickly became well-liked by our Japanese counterparts. He also made many productive customer contacts. Walking into a sushi restaurant with him in Tokyo was quite an experience. He would regale the Japanese sushi chefs behind the counter with some off-color joke in his brand of Japanese and they would burst out laughing. "Mr. Quaiver, very funny man," offered one of our customers.

I invited Steve to join us on one of our trips to Nahodka. As usual, we stayed at the only hotel made available to visitors. I remember it well: small, clean rooms and warm comforters on box beds. The bathtub was made of steel and elevated a foot above the floor, only a few steps from the bed. Bathwater was at best tepid and rust-colored, and taking a bath was not an especially invigorating experience. The room, however, was warm during the frigid winter nights and even warmer during the summer months, owing to the lack of air-conditioning.

The hotel was the center of social activity in this region. Nahodka was the connection point between the trans-Siberian railroad and Japan, as well as a busy cargo port with a thriving fishing industry. On Friday and Saturday evenings, a dance band would begin to play in the hotel's large restaurant, and small groups of locals, mostly single women and men, would arrive and cluster separately by gender at the two dozen or so tables around the dance floor. On this trip, four of us were working on our second bottle of vodka when a large woman approached our table. Quaiver turned to me and exclaimed, "She's looking at you, Art!" The next thing I knew I heard a jumble of Russian, felt the tug of her hand, and was on the dance floor. She was nearly as tall as I and probably weighed the same. She was strongly built, yet at the same time quite feminine, smelling faintly of bath soap and more potently of body odor. However, I found her scent strangely alluring. We didn't dance long, and I wasn't sure which of us was leading. We tried to converse in our respective languages, but soon fell silent. I escorted her back to her table, where three of her girlfriends gawked at me. It was a brief but memorable experience. I had communicated, in a certain way, with an ordinary citizen of the Soviet Union, and clearly a lusty one. "That group of girls is either from a collective farm or one of the factories in this area," commented one of our Russian hosts. "I guess they're trying to find out what an American feels like." he quipped. "Well," I responded, "I feel like I finally got my arms around Mother Russia."

That was on Friday. The next evening a party was held in our honor. Novikov and his small group from Moscow, as well as most of the FESCO managers and their staffs, including a number of women, were present. The venue was an authentic landmark, a huge, ancient ice-breaking tug that had somehow been hauled to the top of a hill and converted into a restaurant and nightclub. The party was a happy event, with a blaring band that could play just about anything. As everyone embraced the party mood, I could sense Steve Quaiver looming over me. "Boss, just watch this. It'll blow your mind. I've asked them to play the tango." Next thing I knew, Steve had a pretty Russian girl in his arms. The dance floor had cleared. In a reincarnation of Rudolph Valentino, Steve floated his partner in a tango step the length of the floor where he abruptly dipped her backward over a table, whipped her around, and floated to the other side of the dance floor to do the same thing, again and again, and back and forth. The Russians loved it. There was a resounding cheer and a heavy dose of clapping in the Russian way, slowly, one clap at a time. Once again, captivated by my Russian hosts and the Russian setting, the Cold War seemed remote.

*   *   *   *

In Mexico City, planning the new Ro-Ro Service to Saudi Arabia (l. to r.) Art, Novikov, and Captain Gonchoro; 1978

International politics were sometimes involved in the pursuit of profitable ventures for MORAM, as they were when we learned of the steamship services provided by the Soviet lines to Cuba, bringing a steady flow of Soviet goods to meet commitments made to Fidel Castro. Large quantities of heavy equipment and vehicles moved to Cuba on specially built Soviet roll-on, roll-off vessels, with side ramps and huge interior decks. The problem was that this trade was essentially one-way, with return cargo limited to bagged sugar. Bill Heffernan called my attention to the potential for MORAM. "Just think of all the commissions we would earn if we could come up with a way to use these vessels on the return voyage." Our shipper contacts told us there was a regular movement of heavy equipment and vehicles from American ports to Saudi Arabia. With the incredible number of building projects underway there, there was a shortage of suitable ship space from the United States, the principal supplier. We enlisted the assistance of Sovinflot in approaching both the Baltic Shipping Company and the Black Sea Shipping Company with a proposal to develop this business, and soon had the approval to go ahead.

MORAM Establishes New RO/RO Department

CLARK, N.J. - The Baltic Shipping Company will inaugurate a regular line RO/RO service beginning January 25 to the Middle East from the U.S. Gulf to Jeddah and Dammam, Arthur C. Novacek, president of MORAM, has announced. MORAM, which will act as agents for the new independent service, has established a RO/RO department to handle the special requirements of the Middle East trade, Novacek said.

U.S. Gulf ports to be used on a regular line basis are Houston and New Orleans. Baltic's large new RO/RO vessel, M/v Magnitogorsk, is scheduled to sail from Houston on January 25 and from New Orleans on January 28. the M/v Komsomolsk will sail from Houston on February 11 and from New Orleans on February 16.

The MORAM official noted that Baltic will be the only RO/RO carrier to offer a regular liner service on this route. Other RO/RO carriers call on Houston and New Orleans on an inducement basis only, Novacek said.

Baltic cargo picked up in the Gulf will be transferred in Rotterdam to fast feeder vessels for direct discharge at Jeddah and Dammam. The first of these feeders is the 18-knot M/v Mekhanik Tarasov, which can carry 100 40-ft. trailers, Novacek said.

The Soviet ro-ro Magnitogorsk is now trading US Gulf/Europe with transshipment to new direct services from Rotterdam to Jeddah and Dammam

"Only one thing," Valeri Novikov cautioned us. "No Soviet citizens are allowed in Saudi Arabia." "I guess we'll have to set up our own agency office there," Bill responded. We established an office in Dubai, close to the Arabian Peninsula, and I hired a former business colleague, Russ Goode, who, aided by his American citizenship, did a commendable job cutting through bureaucratic formalities in both Dubai in the United Arab Emirates, as well as in Saudi Arabia, something the Soviets would never have been able to do. In addition to our regional headquarters in Dubai, we appointed local agents in Jeddah and Damman in Saudi Arabia, and in Dubai, and thus had the distinction of being the only agents representing Soviet Lines at both ends of a trade lane.

*   *   *   *

After those first two difficult years, our organization was functioning well. We had excellent relations with the other agents across the globe. I became comfortable working with the growing number of Soviet principals we represented, and no longer made an effort to avoid letting these relationships be visible with friends and neighbors. An example was a party we gave at my home, a colonial-style house on a tree-lined street in the town of Westfield, New Jersey. The three blocks of Westfield's downtown were graced with a similar style of architecture. It was late spring, and the green, neatly manicured lawns of this historic town gleamed in the sun. The route taken by our Soviet guests would bring them directly through the center of town, past the park with its small lake and stunning white gazebo, sights they would not ordinarily see in their native land.

Two long black limousines rolled up in front of our house, and our seven Soviet guests, all wearing dark suits, stepped out and approached our front door, commenting loudly in Russian as they gaped at the surrounding neighborhood. They joined MORAM executives waiting in our large sunken living room, with its wet bar built into walnut wood cabinets covering an entire wall. Sliding glass doors allowed a full view of the gray slate patio that stretched almost to the two-car garage on the back edge of our property.

My wife had had only two days' notice of the dinner event which was planned to celebrate a visit by George Maslov from Moscow, but we were prepared. We offered plentiful Russian vodka and fine French wines, with a variety of appetizers, followed by steaks and baked potatoes cooked over an outdoor stone grill. Soon the din of many voices in both English and Russian filled the air as our guests spilled out onto the patio. Some of our curious neighbors wandered out in their yards to have a peek. Our five children ventured part-way down the stairs leading to the ground floor, doing their best to see and hear these mysterious beings from Russia. Such curiosity was the nature of things back in the days of the Cold War. Our home and furnishings proved a subject of considerable interest to our Soviet guests. "I would love to have wallpaper like that!" exclaimed Valeri Novikov, admiring the design, a forest of birch trees, on the wall in our dining room. "It would certainly brighten up our apartment in Moscow." In less than a week, rolls of wallpaper with an identical scene were en route to Leningrad on a Baltic Steamship Line vessel. The party was a success, and our relations with Sovinflot were at an all-time high.

We also developed other contacts within the Soviet bureaucracy. This was not difficult, because we were able to entertain Soviet guests in a style pretty much beyond their own means. As an American corporation with our own budget, we considered such entertaining of our principals essential to our success. Once we were asked to help during the visit of the assistant minister of transportation responsible for all Soviet maritime shipping activities. Timofiev, working out of the Sovinflot offices in New York, called me. "Art, you've got to help me. Mr. Stolov is visiting and wants to go fishing. We don't know what to do." "Don't worry, we'll handle it," I replied. "Why not take him to the fishing marina at Sheepshead Bay in Brooklyn? It's well within the 35-mile limit from Columbus Circle," Heffernan suggested. "Sounds good to me, please set that up," I replied, and Heffernan went off to make the arrangements.

It was 6 a.m. on a pleasant sunny day when the limousine pulled up alongside the marina. Out stepped a big florid-faced man with a full head of gray hair, wearing an open-collared dress shirt, gray pin-striped trousers, and dress shoes. "Gentlemen, I'm Stolov *(note: not actual name)*. Where's the fish?" he exclaimed in Russian, or so Captain Timofiev said in translation. We had plenty of beer and vodka and thick Reuben sandwiches. The seas were calm. We hired a 42-foot fishing boat with a good skipper and mate, but couldn't guarantee the fish. Not that we hadn't come up with a plan. We were set up to troll. Four lines trailed the boat. It was agreed that if there were a strike, that rod would be handed to Stolov. Fifteen miles off shore, back and forth the boat went, as we hoped to entice the big ones to our freshly-baited double hooks. Stolov was from the World War II Russian generation, a veteran of the Red Army, his speech, gruff and bombastic. Our conversation stayed on the subject of the merchant marine as we tried to impress him with our superb agency work. Several hours went by along with the consumption of three six-packs of Pilsner, but no fish.

Stolov had only the morning to devote to our fishing venture. We feared impending failure and a very disappointed assistant minister. Suddenly, a rod bent and line whirled off the reel with a screech. At that moment I was sitting in the deck chair closest to the lucky rod and reel. Stolov was standing forward indulging himself with another beer. I grabbed the rod. It was almost yanked out of my hands by the powerful pull of the fish. I started to reel, and was beginning to feel the thrill of the battle. "Give me the damn rod," Heffernan whispered, "You remember the drill," and he thrust it into Stolov's eager hands. Stolov was a skilled angler with plenty of experience fishing in the Baltic Sea outside Leningrad. In about twenty minutes, the mate gaffed a big tuna. We broke out the vodka on the way back to the marina. Toasts abounded. "I don't know how good you are as agents, but at least I know you can find fish," he said. A beaming Stolov climbed into the limo, with wrinkled trousers, scuffed shoes and a bag of filleted tuna.

*   *   *   *

MORAM was making money and our principals were doing well with full cargoes and profitable revenue levels. I had taken a few days vacation to ski with my family. It was noon on a cold, clear day at Mount Tremblant Ski Lodge, ninety miles north of Montreal. Hard-packed snow covered the ski slopes, and my five children and I were crammed into our rented cottage to have lunch. We had removed our ski jackets and were pulling off our sweaters as the air in the room became more humid. We attacked the cheese, bread, and wine and then my daughter held up a slip of paper, "I found this on the night table. Looks like a message for you from your office." The message was from the lodge's front office and read simply "Call your office." "Damn it," I said. "They wouldn't call if it weren't important." I dialed up. "Please put Heffernan on." "Have you been watching television?" Bill asked. "No. I've been skiing all morning," I responded. All was right with the world as far as I was concerned. "Well, brace yourself for this. The Russians have invaded Afghanistan." It took several moments for me to absorb this shocking news. Finally, I replied, "So what," knowing that our government and most Americans would not be happy about this Soviet action. "Well, I've heard through the grapevine that the ILA is threatening to retaliate." As I have mentioned earlier, the ILA, the International Longshoremens Association, was the union that provided labor to work cargo ships at most U.S. East and Gulf Coast ports. I shot back "What gives them the right to do that? They're not a part of our government. It's none of their goddamn business." "Wrong again, mister labor expert," Bill responded. "You know that the ILA is violently opposed to communism and especially the Soviet variety." "OK, OK. Keep me informed," I said as I slammed the phone down. We switched on the TV and soon had a news channel. Soviet tanks were rolling towards Kabul, and the U.S. government had expressed "grave concern over this unwarranted attack."

Today we know the Afghanistan invasion turned out to be the Soviet Union's equivalent of our Vietnam. They were soon bogged down in a quagmire that lasted five years. I talked to Bill every day as I tried to enjoy the remainder of my ski holiday. On the fourth day he said, "Guess what? The ILA has announced that they will not work any Soviet ships other than those already in port or en route." "They can't do that," I insisted. But I knew it was time for me to return and deal with these developments. An avalanche had begun that over the next few weeks would stop us cold. The ILA accomplished in a single action what many competitive steamship lines and the U.S. government had never been able to do: They shut down all the Soviet lines in the U.S. trades by simply refusing to work Soviet vessels.

The Soviets protested through the usual diplomatic channels, but to no avail. Soviet Embassy officials in Washington attempted to arrange a meeting with President Carter to persuade him to intercede, but he declined to see them. An American labor union was dictating U.S. foreign policy, and the Soviet steamship lines were forced to discontinue their U.S. services. In a matter of a few months, I was out of a job.

My time with the Soviets had been one of the most interesting and exciting periods in my business career, despite the reservations I harbored about representing Soviet shipping interests during the Cold War. As is well-known, in the 1980's Soviet Premier Mikhail Gorbachev, General Secretary of the Communist Party and later President of the USSR, ushered in an era of unprecedented reform through *glasnost* and *perestroika*. Glasnost has been defined as an official policy of the former Soviet government emphasizing candor with regard to discussion of social problems and shortcomings. Perestroika has been defined as the restructuring of the Soviet economy and bureaucracy that began in the mid-1980's. These reforms led to the collapse and dissolution of the USSR. I now draw comfort in the belief that my efforts contributed in some measure to this result.

*   *   *   *

POSTSCRIPT

It wasn't until after the demise of the Soviet Union, and the privatization of FESCO, that this once dynamic line resumed some semblance of its global services, primarily between Australia and several U.S. West Coast ports. FESCO remains the biggest regional carrier in the import-export trade in Russia's Far East. It was privatized in December 1992, but privatization had various results, including the loss of shipyards and port businesses, which became independent, private companies. Privatization also left FESCO with a number of non-core businesses, including a brick factory and a sausage factory. FESCO celebrated its 125th anniversary in 2005.

(Source: CONTAINERIZATION INTERNATIONAL, April 2005)

Chapter 10

NAVIERAS de PUERTO RICO

"Some of you know Art Novacek. He's been in this business a long time. Arturo is joining us as President of PRMMI. He will report directly to me, and will be based at our Port Newark office." Thus Roberto Lugo introduced me to the management team of Navieras de Puerto Rico ("Navieras") at their monthly meeting in San Juan in July of 1980. PRMMI was the term commonly used when referring to Puerto Rico Marine Management, Inc., the operating arm of Navieras de Puerto Rico. Navieras was a steamship line owned by the Puerto Rican government, providing container-shipping service between U.S. Atlantic and Gulf ports and San Juan. It had been formed several years earlier when the Puerto Rican government decided that Puerto Rico needed more control over this vital transportation link to insure regular service at reasonable shipping rates. Navieras was formed through the purchase of the assets of three privately-owned steamship lines servicing the Puerto Rican trade: Sea-land, Seatrain and TTT.

Roberto and I were good friends. Twelve years earlier, he had worked for me when I ran Transamerican Trailer Transport (TTT), one of those three privately-owned steamship lines. He had been responsible for all TTT operations in Puerto Rico. Aside from his professional qualifications, he was also active in the political party then in power in Puerto Rico, and a natural choice to become Executive Director of Navieras. During the years I represented Soviet steamship lines, Lugo had urged me to join him at Navieras. I declined his offer for what I thought were good reasons at the time. This was well before the events that led to the forced withdrawal of Soviet steamship lines from the U.S. trades, which left me without a job.

"Hi, Roberto, I guess you heard about the shutdown of Soviet steamship services. I was wondering if you would reconsider the job offer you made several years ago?" I asked, groveling on the phone to Roberto in San Juan. There was a disconcerting pause. "Well, you know, Arturo, it's been some time since then. I've managed to adjust our organization and I am just not sure what I can do now. Let me work on it and get back to you." This was an entirely reasonable response under the circumstances. At the time, though, I was getting close to the panic stage. One of my weaknesses is a lack of patience, and I was no different then. I couldn't sit back and calmly appraise the situation, take my time, and see what job opportunities might develop. I wanted another good job "right now." I had not been without a job a single day since I graduated from Kings Point thirty years earlier. Several days went by without a return call from Roberto. I called back. "Is Roberto there?" "No, he's in a meeting, and he can't be disturbed." I tried again several more times during the following week. Nothing. Finally, "Arturo, sorry I didn't get back to you, I had some things to work out. I'm ready to go ahead, and look forward to you joining Navieras. Fly down to San Juan and let's work out the arrangements. There's a management meeting coming up in a couple of days, so the timing is good." Several days prior to the meeting, Lugo and I negotiated an agreement. I would serve as president and chief operating officer of PRMMI, reporting directly to him, with the senior officers of PRMMI, both those in Puerto Rico and on the mainland reporting to me. I executed a contract confirming my position as president and COO. There were ten senior vice presidents, four in San Juan and six in the U.S.

The senior managers at the meeting were a mixture of Puerto Ricans and mainland Americans. Puerto Ricans are American citizens, but since Puerto Rico is a United States commonwealth and not a state, Puerto Ricans do not vote in our Presidential elections. I sat to the right of Lugo at a long gleaming conference table at Navieras headquarters in the Hato Rey section of San Juan. There were about a dozen men present, and those from the mainland always adjusted their schedules to be available for the monthly meetings. All flew First Class and stayed in the best hotels in San Juan. I quickly got into the swing of things, and did the same. My preferred hotel was the Caribe Hilton, where my favorite receptionist would greet me with "The tower, the tower! Welcome, Mr. Novacek. Yes, I know, you want a room in the tower." The air-conditioning worked better in the tower rooms, and so did the elevators serving the upper floors. The Caribe also served a good breakfast buffet and had one of the finest restaurants in San Juan for lunch or dinner, that is, if I wasn't eating at one of the other superb restaurants in San Juan.

There was usually a long agenda, with Lugo in the chair. That first meeting droned on all day, with a brief time-out for lunch at a nearby restaurant. To impress everyone at the meeting, I took voluminous notes. When the others made no effort to do so, it should have sounded a warning bell. "And now," Lugo said, "we have to address escalating overhead costs. We're still not showing a profit, and it seems to me that we may be overstaffed." The heads around him nodded in agreement. Some of those heads belonged to my mainland managerial staff. "I'd like to set a target of a 10 percent reduction in headcount. How does that sound to you?" The heads nodded again. "Can you do it with the mainland staff, Art?" I actually didn't have a clue at that point. "Why not?" I responded and my head went up and down with the others.

Back in Port Newark, I gathered my six head-nodding staffers. "OK, you heard the man. Let's get to it." But suddenly their heads stilled. One manager lamented, "I'm stretched thin already, so how do you expect me to do it?" It took me until the next management meeting in San Juan to achieve a 7 percent reduction, by attrition, layoffs, and staffing adjustments. I was proud of myself, sitting next to Lugo, impatiently waiting for the subject of staffing to come up on the agenda. The hours came and went, but the topic of layoffs was never mentioned. When the meeting ended, and I was walking out with him, I inquired, "Didn't you miss something? What about staffing reductions?" "Oh, yeah, Arturo, I meant to tell you. We have a lot of unemployment in Puerto Rico, and the governor's office found out about our plans. Word came back, 'no layoffs.' In fact, I've had some calls pushing me to add staff. You know how politics are."

Frankly, at that time I *didn't* know, at least, not about Puerto Rican politics. For example, in those days, Puerto Rico had a voting turnout of more than 90 percent in gubernatorial elections, and a large proportion of the population worked for the government. There were two major political parties, and the winner of the governorship filled numerous government jobs with his or her supporters, while the losing party fought to keep its supporters on board. I soon learned to play the game, although it always troubled me since we were, indeed, overstaffed. What a way to run a business. Well, it really wasn't a business, but a branch of government, and "whoever heard of one of those being run efficiently?" I thought.

Navieras de Puerto Rico had two strikes against it from its inception. When the Puerto Rico Maritime Shipping Authority (PRMSA) bought out the Puerto Rican service of three existing privately-owned shipping companies servicing the island, Navieras incurred a debt running into millions of dollars. Any profits from operations were easily usurped by the magnitude of the company's debt service. Lugo was still struggling with the lack of proper capitalization when I departed the company in 1983.

JOURNAL OF COMMERCE, **June 7, 1983**

Navieras Asks Gov't For $100 Million Grant

Journal of Commerce Special

SAN JUAN — Although maritime cargo tonnage to and from Puerto Rico has improved slightly in the past two years, Navieras de Puerto Rico, the island's government-owned shipping line, is facing stiff competition from private companies and a lack of capital to maintain and improve its service.

Navieras is reported to have a share of about 60 percent of the island's maritime trade, but its operational losses and lack of capital, since it was purchased in 1974, are hurting its prospects.

In his latest annual report, Roberto Lugo D'Acosta, Navieras' executive director, explains the situation thus:

"Imports from the U.S. mainland, Navieras' principal source of cargo, dropped by 4.1 percent from the already low fiscal 1981 level, while

If freight rates are not increased for the coming fiscal year, he says, Navieras is expected to lose $39.1 million, provided the present volume of cargo is maintained. He suggested a 6.5 percent freight rate increase.

Mr. Lugo has predicted that in the next 20 years Navieras may accumulate obligations of about $800 million, on the basis of present commitments.

Navieras' management has mentioned competition as one of its main problems, since it has been losing part of its market share to private shipping companies such as TMT and Sea-Land.

Competition by TMT and Sea-Land is far stiffer now than when Navieras was organized in 1974 by buying out the Puerto Rican services of Sea-Land, Seatrain, and Trans America Trailer Transport. The merger of these lines and their equipment gave Navieras an 80 percent share of the cargo shipments

The opposition party had a heyday. *Navieras Shows Another Loss,* the headlines screamed. It was a tough situation to deal with, since the governor in power had supported the creation of Navieras. Even worse, the deal made with two of the three companies whose assets had been acquired, Sea-Land Service and Crowley Maritime, permitted them to resume their Puerto Rican operations after a very short time. Both were large, international shipping lines, and this short delay posed no problem for them as they rounded up the necessary vessels and container equipment and prepared to reenter the trade. Soon they were back in full swing, and the monopoly years for Navieras ended.

When I arrived on the scene, the competition was fierce between the state-owned line and the two private operators. It was no surprise that the privately-owned lines were getting the best of it, increasing their market share. My major contribution, in the three years I was there, was establishing a professional marketing program to generate new revenues. Lugo let me run with that segment of the business, which he knew was my forte. Until then, Navieras's marketing and sales program had lacked clear goals and focus. Bernie Carr, then senior vice president of marketing, was a good-looking guy with silver hair, about my age, and he came from the old wine-and-dine school. "Art, how about joining us for lunch?" and off we'd go to a pricey Italian restaurant in Lower Manhattan to meet the export traffic manager of, let's say, Union Carbide. That's when I could still handle martinis, or presumed so. The problem was that Union Carbide was not a big shipper to Puerto Rico. The traffic manager, however, was an old friend of Bernie's, and we did get his business, what little there was of it. At that time, Navieras did not maintain a databank of information on shipments made either with Navieras or with the competition, and consequently didn't know the volume or type of cargo shipped by each active shipper, making it difficult to identify potential clients and to determine their cargo volumes.

I also turned my attention to marketing and public relations, and was fortunate to find on staff an English major who was an accomplished writer and had a flair for promotion. Roberta Greening, vivacious and attractive, was the editor and writer of a company in-house newsletter, *SHIP'S BELL,* which was crammed with company wide news-bits and a favorite of the employees. In a short time, she became manager of the company's corporate communications. Teaching her some of the requirements of a business was another matter. The first time I requested a budget report, she did not respond right away. A day or so later, she appeared at my office door. "What exactly is in a budget report?" she asked nervously, and I obliged by spelling out the basics. After that she would go on to do a very good job for the company. In fact, she would later found one of the leading public relations firms in the maritime industry, representing a number of companies in cargo shipping and related concerns.

My approach to marketing was the same one I had used to set up programs in my past jobs. I didn't invent it, but it worked each time. I set up statistical data by shipper both southbound to Puerto Rico and northbound to U.S. mainland ports. This information allowed us to assign accounts to our salesmen in a logical way and to arm them with

PRMMI Has New President
Arthur C. Novacek Joins Executive Staff

Effective July 23, Arthur C. Novacek joined PRMMI/Navieras as President & Chief Operating Officer. All regional Executive Vice Presidents and the Senior Vice Presidents of Traffic, Marketing and Vessel Operations will report directly to Mr. Novacek who will be domiciled in the Elizabeth port.

Mr. Novacek brings with him a wealth of experience in the maritime industry. His most recent position was as President of Moram Agencies, Inc., the U.S. general agent for Russia's Far East Shipping Co. Prior to that, he had worked as President Container Division for Seatrain Lines, and President of Grace Lines.

Instrumental in the formation of Transamerican Trailer Transport (TTT) in 1966, Mr. Novacek served as the first Executive Vice President and General Manager of that Company. His earlier experience in the shipping industry included both marketing and traffic responsibilities.

After graduating from the U.S. Merchant Marine Academy at Kings Point, New York, Mr. Novacek served three years in the U.S. Navy during the Korean War. He then continued his education by attending night classes at New York University where he received an M.B.A. degree.

Originally from Omaha, Nebraska, Mr. Novacek currently resides in Westfield, New Jersey. He and his wife, Jeanette, have five children, four sons and a daughter.

An avid jogger, Mr. Novacek runs 4 - 5 miles at least four times a week. He maintains this schedule even when traveling. He also enjoys

Arthur C. Novacek, President and Chief Operating Officer.

reading, and tries to read one or two books a week. While jogging is his primary leisure activity, he does play an occasional round of golf.

Enthusiastic about his new responsibilities at PRMMI/Navieras, Mr. Novacek has been busily engaged in formulating his goals and objectives to enhance the future of PRMMI/Navieras. His expertise and vast experience in the maritime industry should lend itself well to accomplishing these plans.

by R. L. Greening, Personnel/Elizabeth

Navieras Participates in Expoferia 80

On June 11-16, the First International Fair of Industry and Commerce, or Expoferia 80, was held at the Roberto Clemente Coliseum in San Juan, Puerto Rico. Navieras was well represented at the fair with a display booth and hospitality suite. Eleven members of our San Juan Marketing staff were on hand to inform the public about our service.

Expoferia 80 was organized by Expoferras de Puerto Rico, Inc., to promote commerce and industry in Puerto Rico, as well as to encourage international trade. This was the first of the annual fairs scheduled to take place in June each year.

Open to the public on weekdays from 12:30 P.M. to 9:30 P.M., the fair featured displays from all types of service and manufacturing companies. Navieras took this excellent opportunity to make our present and potential customers aware of our trade routes and the equipment available to serve the island of Puerto Rico.

by A. de La Rosa, Personnel/San Juan

Puerto Rico Marine Management's house organ, The SHIP's BELL, August 1980

valuable data on volumes shipped and carriers used. By then, Puerto Rico was well-grounded in the capitalist system. In 1952, Puerto Rico achieved Commonwealth status with a proper constitution, and residents were also exempted from federal income taxes. In 1954, the U.S. government established incentives whereby U.S. multinationals enjoyed lucrative federal tax credits on profits earned by their manufacturing subsidiaries in Puerto Rico. Mainland U.S. manufacturers had rushed to establish plants in Puerto Rico, and there were now hundreds of privately-owned small businesses and dozens of subsidiaries and branches of large American firms in the country. Navieras had sales offices on the mainland and in Puerto Rico, and I usually spent several days a month in

(l. to r.) "Mikki" Diaz, Roberto Lugo, Art, and Froilan Ansa at a going-away party for Art in San Juan, May, 1983

both places, meeting with our sales people and accompanying them on sales calls. Roberto Lugo had managed to assemble a cast of colorful and, in most cases, capable managers in Puerto Rico. One, a local sports hero, was about my height, six-two, and small for a forward, but, when he was a young man, good enough to make the Puerto Rican national basketball team. It was curious that Puerto Rico had its own representation in the Olympics, even though it is a commonwealth of the United States.

Of course, Puerto Rico has its own language and culture, and Puerto Ricans are proud of both. For example, the ex-basketball player, Froilan Ansa, Navieras executive vice president, Caribbean, had responsibility for the company's sales program in Puerto Rico. With the long, dark features and drooping mustache of his Basque heritage, he had an "oh, shucks" modesty and wry smile, and was equally liked by his staff and his many customers. The Spanish language did not come easily to me, especially the Puerto Rican Spanish, but I'd swear that Ansa spoke it with a drawl. He had a great sense of humor and referred to me as "The Machine." I asked him about the name one day and he responded with a question of his own. Why do you think I gave you that name?" "Don't kid me," I said. "I don't particularly like it." Actually, I considered it funny and probably appropriate, since I was work-driven wherever I was, constantly meeting with customers and conducting reviews with our sales staff.

*   *   *   *

"Where did it go?" asked Roberto. "See that bush over there, about ten feet back from the big palm?" replied Miguel ("Mikki") Diaz. He had done it again. It took an ex-caddy, scratch golfer, and current vice president of PRMMI to locate one of our golf balls. Lugo was unusually skilled in spotting management and leadership talent among his Puerto Rican associates, then assigning them to key executive positions. Mikki Diaz was not just a great golf partner and excellent player, but an outstanding manager as well. His specialty was container operations, particularly container repair and maintenance. He eventually became the Navieras executive vice president, southeast region, based in Jacksonville, Florida. He was born and raised in a poor section of San Juan and picked himself up by the bootstraps, caddying at one of the exclusive golf clubs as an early step along his career path.

Navieras Golf Outing (l. to r.) Art, Mikki Diaz, Governor Carlos Romero Barcelo and far right, Roberto Lugo; 1982

"Hey, Arturo! You're squeezing that club handle to death. Loosen up," he'd shout, as I sliced another ball into the rough. Mikki not only helped me with my golf game, he gave me insight into the Puerto Rican psyche. His almost black eyes would brighten and his smile widened whenever I met him. Of medium height, he had the trim, athletic look of someone who could, and did, scuba-dive for long hours on weekends. He had a close relationship with Lugo, and would firmly hold his ground in any discussion. Sometimes, at informal social events, he would wear a narrow-brimmed straw-colored hat with a wide band, replete with a small feather adornment; and a silk sport shirt splashed with primary colors. His pressed white linen trousers would complete his look. If there was music playing, especially a mamba, Mikki would be the first one on the dance floor.

Lugo didn't fare quite as well with the Puerto Rican executives he positioned on the mainland, and sometimes it was hard for them to adjust. Francisco (Frank) Rodriguez, for example, was a graduate of the University of Puerto Rico and had done his graduate studies in the U.S. with a specialty of computer science. While on a consulting contract with Navieras, he had impressed Lugo with his intelligence and dedication. When I arrived on the scene, Frank had already been appointed Navieras executive vice president, Gulf & West Coast, based in New Orleans.

"Don Roberto, how do you think we should handle this matter?" was a typical approach from Frank Rodriguez to Lugo. The honorary title "Don" surprised me the first time I heard Rodriguez use it. For a moment, I felt as if I was back in the days of the Spanish colonial Puerto Rico, and Roberto was the owner of a prosperous sugar cane plantation. Rodriguez typified the upper tier social status of old Puerto Rico, where a small upper-class dominated the social and economic scene. I also thought that he was fawning on Lugo, who, incidentally, never corrected him. In fact, I thought Lugo rather liked the idea of being Don Roberto. Lugo's father had at one time been an itinerant Baptist minister, and he served as a fine example of a Puerto Rican professional who succeeded on his own merits. He too was a graduate of the University of Puerto Rico. Educated and trained as a C.P.A., he had been a business executive for as long as I had known him.

Still, Lugo looked and acted the part of a Don. One year older than I, he had long, wavy, gray hair accentuated by thick, dark eyebrows, full lips, and a sturdy physique. His English could at times be stilted, and I found myself offering help when he seemed to falter on occasion. He was thoughtful and reasonable in his dealings with his managers, and often turned to me for advice. What he prized most from his subordinates was loyalty, and he reciprocated in kind.

Over time, Frank Rodriguez had difficulty in grasping and acting on day-to-day operating needs, so much so that he finally withdrew from his responsibilities altogether and refused to come to his office. Since Frank had a direct reporting relationship to me, I made several trips to New Orleans trying to help him in his dealings with his mainland staff, all experienced local talent, with whom he could not always comfortably relate. The situation showed little improvement.

I was finally successful in convincing Lugo that Frank simply could not adjust to the requirements of his job in New Orleans, and was more suited to the work he had previously done as a computer consultant. But rather than terminating Frank or demoting him, Lugo created a new position of senior vice president, administration, and brought him back to Puerto Rico to join his staff in San Juan, where, in reality, the previous administrative director continued to perform the duties the position required.

*   *   *   *

Robert Magee was an outstanding senior executive who Lugo recruited from Sun Shipbuilding in Chester, Pennsylvania, where the Navieras' Ro/Ro vessels were constructed. Magee, 33 at the time, a Kings Point graduate, was a highly regarded manager at Sun. Lugo appointed him senior vice president, corporate vessel operations, and the company relocated him to San Juan. At first glance, with his boyish features, Bob looked out of place among the executives who gathered in San Juan for the monthly managers' meetings, but he quickly made a lasting impression on me with his unerring

175

knowledge of the Navieras fleet, which, at the time consisted of both aging containerships and the more sophisticated Ro/Ro vessels.

NAVIERAS joins American Ships Display at the Smithsonian Museum in Washington, DC, by donating a photo of a roll-on/roll-off vessel. (l. to r.) Bob Magee, a Smithsonian official, and Art, 1983.

After departing from Navieras, Magee went on to join Totem Ocean Trailer Express (TOTE), which successfully operates similar Ro/Ro vessels in the U.S. coastal trade with Alaska. He rose to the position of chairman, president, and CEO of American Shipping Group, the holding company of TOTE and also Sea Star Line.

(Related information can be found in the Postscript to Chapter 4, TTT, page 74.)

*   *   *   *

Lugo had a sensitive assignment as a major fundraiser for Governor Carlos Romero-Barcelo. Navieras de Puerto Rico had a host of vendors who were expected to make thank-you political contributions when asked. Lugo had an aide, "Pepe" Fraga, whose principal task was to coordinate fund-raising activities. He was well-suited to the job. A tough-looking former bodyguard for the deposed dictator of Cuba, Fulgencio Batista, Pepe brought a special energy to the position and was particularly effective in leaning on the sometimes reluctant contributors. As an important cog in the fund-raising process, Lugo had direct access to the Governor. The amiable Carlos Romero would even attend major social functions or join in golf outings for important customers of Navieras. Lugo was able to juggle the political requirements of his position at Navieras with the company's business needs very effectively.

The Board of Directors of Navieras was appointed by the Governor. I was invited by Lugo to attend most of the board meetings for the purpose of reporting on the progress of the business. The first of these meetings I attended held a unique surprise for me, one which had nothing to do with our business at hand. The board membership was a mixture of politicians, lawyers, and even a pharmacist who owned a chain of drug stores across the island. Already present when they arrived, I was greeted in a very friendly way as the token "gringo" at their meetings.

Whole pig barbecuing in the foreground at Lugo's mountain retreat at a fund-raiser for Governor Romero September,1981. (l. to r.) Art, Mikki Diaz, Bernie Carr, Roberto Lugo, Joan Carr

When we sat down to business, each man placed his briefcase on the table and opened it up. As the case lids rose, I couldn't believe my eyes. Almost all of the men had handguns casually resting on top of their papers and work files. I had never seen so much hardware in one room before, and much less in a business conference room. I would soon learn that this was not an uncommon practice in Puerto Rico, although one that I personally chose not to adopt. It also gave me some indication of the state of law enforcement in San Juan, where, in the early 1980s, muggings were common. This has since been corrected, however, to protect the island's strong and growing tourism business.

Lugo constantly catered to the special needs of his directors, which often meant finding a job for a director's relatives. In some ways, he was like the stereotypical Mafia Don, with his own chauffer, bodyguard, and a full entourage responding to his whims; and with his connections to the Governor, he was actually a part of a greater power structure on the island.

I took my regular early-morning jogs along the winding and sometimes cobblestone streets of San Juan on a route that was always the same: out the long driveway from the Hilton, then a right turn onto the shoreline road, up the long hill, past the massive yellow-brick Capitol building which rested across the street from a high cliff overlooking the Caribbean Sea. I then passed El Morro, the huge landmark fortress that dates back to the time of the Spanish galleons, and as far as Old San Juan, with its main square lined with pastel colonial buildings boasting grated wrought iron balcony railings and window covers, before retracing my steps.

These runs allowed me plenty of time to reflect on the strange situation in which I found myself, working for a government that, owing to Puerto Rico's commonwealth status, was democratically elected. I thought that if Puerto Rico had not come under U.S. control after the Spanish-American War, it would likely be as much inclined to dictatorship as any of its Caribbean neighbors. Navieras, like every other Puerto Rican government entity, with its many politically appointed employees, faced the election prospect of "Out with the losers, in with the winners." So my tenure at Navieras hinged upon Carlos Romero's winning the coming election.

It was a long night as I lay on my bed at the Caribe Hilton, watching election results on TV. I had been at Navieras less than a year, and was as nervous about the outcome of the gubernatorial election as any of the other senior executives in our organization. The election was very closely fought and I wasn't fully convinced when Lugo had remarked, "We have nothing to worry about, Arturo. We should win this one hands down." I didn't feel much like trying to find another job so soon, and, besides, this was a pretty easy way to live and work, with everything first-class, good pay, and even some time on the beach to enjoy the Caribbean sun. The election results on TV were nerve-wracking, with the lead swinging back and forth during the night. It wasn't until late in the morning that Romero's opponent conceded. Good, I had another two years to go before the next election.

Art and Roberto, 1982

Airline travel to San Juan could be interesting. Several times I flew in Tourist Class when First Class was full. The tourist cabin was crowded with Puerto Ricans of all sizes and shapes, and the baggage racks were chock-a-block with their bundles and luggage. Often their carry-on consisted of food and groceries that would give the compartment a unique odor, reminiscent of a hallway in an old apartment building, where the smell of breakfast bacon and eggs could be mixed with the scent of a corned beef and cabbage dinner. Always expressive, the native Puerto Ricans would fill the plane with a clamor that echoed a busy street festival. It was only about a four-hour flight from Newark Airport, but sometimes it seemed twice that long. The first time I landed in San Juan, I was shocked by the applause that marked the plane's successful touch-down. Those who had checked baggage would find a mass of bodies engulfing the baggage carousel as yet another torrent of bags and boxes of all sizes would tumble out. About as many Puerto Ricans lived in the New York area as in San Juan, and for each one arriving in San Juan, there were at least a half dozen greeters.

It was up to me to find a taxi, hopefully air-conditioned, and head off to the Caribe Hilton. The air was usually thick with humidity and heat but the scenic ride made up for it. I enjoyed passing the housing projects, where all manner of activities were taking place: pick-up basketball games, rough and tumble kids playing catch with old tennis balls, even some strolling prostitutes. Sometimes the taxi would pass horse-drawn carts. Eventually we would roll past suburban homes as we approached the Condado Beach area and its line of oceanfront resort hotels. Finally the taxi would cross the low, flat, four-lane bridge that connects the Condado area with the Hilton, where I was staying, and beyond to Old San Juan. After a right turn onto the palm-lined driveway and a wait in the check-in line, I would finally reach the cool comfort of my tower room, so cool that I usually slept in the long-sleeved shirt I had worn during the day.

The arrival experience at the San Juan airport was much the same as at Santo Domingo or Trinidad, with the main difference being the absence of immigration clearance at San Juan, since flights from the U.S. were domestic, not international. I had occasion to visit those other countries, as well as St. Thomas in the U.S. Virgin Islands and Port-au-Prince, the capital of Haiti, since Navieras provided container cargo service to all four by small feeder ships via San Juan.

I took a particular interest in this island service, since a new set of customers was involved and the competition included lines calling directly from U.S. ports. Moreover, Navieras agents in these countries were quite different from our managers in Puerto Rico. With the exception of the government entity that we partnered with in Trinidad, these agents were relatively small, locally-owned companies. Our use of such agents rather than establishing Navieras branch offices produced significant savings, since by doing so we avoided the expense of setting up and staffing a new facility, and also reaped the benefits of any long-standing customer relations these local agents had already established through their representation of European steamship lines.

The trade between mainland U.S. ports and Puerto Rico is covered by the Jones Act (Section 27 of the Merchant Marine Act of 1920), which governs the transportation by water of cargo between two domestic points by reserving such cargo to U.S-owned, U.S.-built, and U.S.-manned vessels. Therefore, foreign-flag vessels cannot compete in the mainland U.S.-Puerto Rican trade. But no such restriction applies to trade between the mainland U.S. or Puerto Rico and any Caribbean nation. The consequence is that shipping costs are generally higher in the Puerto Rican trades because of the substantially greater expense of building and manning American ships. (The same is true in the shipping lanes between mainland ports and Hawaii and Alaska.) A principal purpose of the Jones Act is to ensure the availability of American-Flag vessels in time of war, but it also serves to benefit intra-American shipping of all kinds.

"Walito, what's that framed document on the wall behind your desk?" I asked Waldo Heinsen, the owner of our agency in Santo Domingo. "Don't you recognize the signature?" he responded. "No, why, should I?" "That's the order appointing my father as Consul General for the German Reich in Santo Domingo, and it's signed by Adolph Hitler. My dad was a German immigrant to this country in the late 1920's, started his own agency company, and eventually became agents for the steamship service of Hamburg-Sud." With his ample girth, Walito looked the picture of a big beer-drinking Bavarian, except for his dark complexion inherited from his mother, a Dominican. He had all the Prussian traits of his forefathers, and ran a tight ship. His son, "Teddy" Heinsen was quite the opposite: slender, flexible in both body and personality, and ready to learn the needs of a strong marketing program in his country as assistant to his father.

Walito's counterpart in Haiti, Lionel D'Adesky, was a Belgian immigrant who had married well in Haiti and, with help from his wife, had built and owned his own business, engaging in a number of shipping-related activities. His son-in-law, Wilhelm "Wikki" Lemke, was slender like Teddy Heinsen, but with blond hair and blue eyes, and had in his father-in-law a more lenient employer than Teddy had in his father. Both Lionel and Wikki were fluent in the native Creole language and managed to prosper in a somewhat hostile environment. Lionel owned a home in the foothills outside Port-au-Prince which I always viewed as a smaller version of the Fontainebleau Hotel at Miami Beach. It was a wonderful place to unwind with a martini in the early evening, often with the sound of voodoo drums and melodies somewhere in the distance. The difference between Lionel's lifestyle and that of the Haitian populace was striking, but he had good relationships with the government and the workers he employed, which suggested to me that he shared his wealth in the right places at the right time.

Although there was a small middle-class in Haiti largely employed in business, there was an enormous gap between the lower classes, more than 99 percent of Haiti's population, and D'Adesky and his wealthy friends. It was disturbing to me, sitting on the pool-deck veranda of my hotel, no more than 15 minutes from D'Adesky's home, to look down on unimaginable poverty: shacks with castoff corrugated roofs and walls of warped plywood, no running water or electricity, and half-starved pigs rooting in refuse scattered on the narrow dirt roads. It was hard to imagine that Haiti had once been the wealthiest of all French colonies, with great plantations and broad expanses of leafy trees and tropical plants. Now there was virtually no forest left and firewood was non-existent except in the country's interior.

D'Adesky's class, by virtue of its wealth, controlled the country's business and banking. This was the time of "Baby Doc," Jean Claude, the son who had succeeded his father, Francois "Papa Doc" Duvalier, as dictator. The elder Duvalier was the creator of the infamous Tontons Macoute, a private militia that had terrorized the population, but seemed to appear from out of nowhere when a visiting businessman or tourist encountered a problem with the locals. On one occasion, when my then eighteen-year old daughter, Jill, was with me on vacation from the University of Vermont, we decided to visit the famous citadel, La Ferrière, the fortress built in the early seventeenth century by

Henri Christophe near Cap-Haïtien on the northern coast of Haiti. Our plan was to ascend to the crumbling ruins by mountain pony.

After a long road trip from Port-au-Prince in the car loaned us by Lionel and an overnight in a local hotel, we drove as far as we could up the rock-strewn approach, with the hope of hiring ponies and a guide. Suddenly we were besieged by a group of local guides with ponies, demanding our business. Just as suddenly, three authoritative and imposing men dressed in the typical outfits of the Tontons Macoute, long-sleeved white shirts and dark trousers, materialized. In a matter of two or three minutes we had two ponies and two guides, at reasonable prices, and were on our way. I doubt that this would happen in today's Haiti.

In May of 1983, Navieras agents in the Caribbean gave Art a Departure Party held in San Juan (l. to r.) Robertito Lugo, Waldo Heinsen, Rudy Francis, Wikki Lemke, Carol Francis, Art, Teddy Heinsen, Rosa Fernandez, Lionel D'Adesky, and Froilan Ansa

*   *   *   *

The Georgia quail-hunting expedition had been arranged by Lorenzo Santiago, the Navieras executive vice president of the Southeast Region, and another of Lugo's Puerto Rican protégés. Lorenzo was my height, outweighing me by about 40 pounds, with a full face, and a thick, dark mustache. He always wore dark glasses when he was outdoors, sun or no sun. He was friendly and ingratiating with his superiors, but had difficulty dealing with his mainland staff who viewed him as overbearing, which was not hard to do, given his height and girth and loud, demanding voice. Only about 35, Lorenzo had a quick mind and could be persuasive in Spanish, qualities I'm sure that had attracted him to Lugo. With little previous managerial experience, he tried to make up in bluster what he lacked in confidence. I no longer recall what precipitated it, but not many months after our quail-hunting weekend, Santiago was transferred to Port Newark as the Navieras executive vice president, Northeast Region, in offices not far from my own. The idea was that I could provide him with more personal support and direction. Once again, Lugo had protected and was loyal to his hand-picked senior executives.

A mixture of customers and Navieras executives, we had been driven by chartered bus the previous afternoon from our meeting point in Jacksonville to the hunting lodge outside Macon, Georgia. Most of the customers were seasoned hunters and all brought their favorite shotguns, several with engraved bronze identification plates. I borrowed

one, scratched and weathered, from the lodge. Lorenzo had been taking shooting lessons at a local skeet facility in Jacksonville, home of our regional office, where he lived. I had little experience with a shotgun, strange for a farm boy from Nebraska. The dogs would find the quail, then freeze in position with their tails held rigidly in the air, nose pointed toward the covey hidden in the brush. It was up to the hunters to flush them and pick out a whirring target as the quail flew up in all directions.

Robbie, Art, and Lorenzo ready to hunt quail in Georgia

184

This is the standard procedure, but it was my first quail hunt and all new to me.

"Hey Frank," I whispered to the lodge-owner and our hunting guide, "Do you suppose you could take me down to your range so I could get a little practice with this weapon?" I wanted it to be a private session, just him and me, but Frank missed the point as he bellowed, "Anyone want to join Art and me for some practice?" It was the afternoon of our arrival, and off we trooped to the range, Frank and I and five others. "OK Art, I'll work the machine and you're first up." Before I could even set up, the clay pigeon was flying across the field. I missed and the sailing clay disk disappeared into the grass. I repeated my failure on my next four tries. Meanwhile, my colleagues were scattering clay right and left as they took their turns. Humbled by my poor shooting, I hoped that luck would intervene over the next two days to restore a bit of personal pride. It never occurred to me that something other than shooting quail would happen the next day where some personal expertise with a shotgun might have helped.

It was a chilly morning as the ten of us formed a long line across the grounds of the quail-hunting resort, a Georgia plantation. The temperature proved to be some of that luck when, after no more than fifteen steps into the thick grass, my foot brushed something that felt like a rotting log. I stopped abruptly, looked down, and immediately lifted my right foot, barely touching the ground. (I was glad I was wearing the lower leg protection pads Lorenzo had given me.) Lethargic from the cold, the rattlesnake was slow to react. It emerged sluggishly from the ground-cover of dead pine needles, its thick body coiled and those perilous jaws, now opened, only a foot or two from my motionless right leg. I heard a whisper, "Stand steady, Art." I hadn't noticed Robbie Harrison's approach from behind. One loud report from Robbie's shotgun and the snake's head was in tatters. Robbie was a member of our group and an expert shot. Later, when the rattler was hung on a post in front of the lodge, it measured almost six feet in length; its body as thick as my upper arm.

*   *   *   *

The feeder services that Navieras provided via San Juan to four other Caribbean Islands were a very different operation from the regular mainland services, and needed special direction. The small roll-on roll-off feeder ships used were all chartered foreign-flag vessels that required close daily operating attention in order to make timely connections with the mainline vessels at San Juan, and also quick turn-around in Santo Domingo, Puerto-au-Prince, Trinidad, and St. Thomas. Each of these ports was served by a different feeder, with the St. Thomas service actually provided by a tug-barge unit due to the close proximity of the two ports. Lugo and I concluded that the operations department could not provide the direction and control essential to these specialized feeder operations. Suddenly, "Arturo, you've had an opportunity to observe Robertito, and can see that he is a hard-working, sharp young man." (Robertito, Lugo's youngest son, had been languishing in a terminal-management position in San Juan.) "He's very impressive," I responded, and diplomatically continued in the same vein, "I was thinking we should create the position of an operations director devoted to running these feeders. This would be a good opportunity for Robertito to show what he can do."

Robertito was not quite 30, and at that point had had little management experience. Nevertheless, I liked the idea. Lugo wasn't completely sold on the feeder concept and my logic was that the success of this segment of the business was largely in my hands and how better to get the tools I needed, ships and staff, than with the support of the son of the executive director of the whole shebang? We were off and running as I concentrated on marketing these services, even creating a separate sales group, while Robertito, based in San Juan, provided operational direction. The father-son approach wasn't always easy, as witnessed by our efforts in Trinidad. I was successful in working out a unique arrangement with the Trinidadian government which, taking a page out of the Puerto Rican book, created a government-owned steamship company. The same rationale for this new entity was given as had been advanced in Puerto Rico: the need to assure good ocean-shipping service to the island country at reasonable freight rates.

The deal between the two governments covered cargo moving between U.S. ports and Trinidad, with containers being shipped to San Juan on Navieras vessels, then transferred to a feeder vessel provided by a government-owned company equivalent to Navieras. Revenues would be split fifty-fifty, with all expenses on the move between U.S. ports and San Juan the responsibility of Navieras, and those incurred between San Juan and Trinidad the responsibility of the Trinidadian company. That was simple enough, but it was an accountant's nightmare to keep track of the numbers needed to determine financial results. It was Navieras' responsibility to handle all sales in both the U.S. and Trinidad; and, therefore, we had to select an agent in Trinidad. I was pretty well along in working out an arrangement with a well-established agency company when Robertito, who was diligently working on the operating aspects of this new service, established a personal relationship with a trucker in Trinidad who provided pickup and delivery of containers locally. Robertito thought that this trucker, young and aggressive like himself, and by now his good friend, could set up an agency department and do that work as well, but I told him that I would prefer to use an experienced agent.

"Arturo, do you have a few minutes?" I was in San Juan at the time, and, as I sat in Roberto's office, I wasn't quite sure what was up. "Robertito's been keeping me advised of developments in Trinidad. Seems he feels strongly about giving his trucker friend an opportunity. I think we should support him. It will give him the confidence he needs in his new job." I tried to point out in a diplomatic way that it wasn't up to the operating man to appoint agents who would largely be performing marketing activities, and that we needed a firm with good customer contacts. But Lugo's proven loyalty to his Puerto Rican executive appointments applied equally to his son. I didn't make an issue of it, but was thoroughly embarrassed in my further dealings in Trinidad. Three months later, we were obliged to turn the agency work over to my original selection, since the trucker wasn't working out. "Robertito," Roberto Jr., was a taller, darker version of his father, intelligent and dedicated. In time, I would become one of his principal mentors, which he acknowledges to this day.

*   *   *   *

From a roller-coaster ride managing a steamship agency owned by the Soviet Union, to a lesson in diplomacy working with a steamship line owned by the Puerto Rican government, I had gone through a major transition. Reporting directly to Roberto Lugo gave me the opportunity to continue my career in a dignified manner. Over a period of three years I was able to take stock, and, at age 55, to examine my options for the future. I had learned from the last gubernatorial election in Puerto Rico that the future of Navieras would be decided in less than a year when another election would take place.

It was early in 1983 that the call came in from an executive-search firm, with the news that I was being considered for the position of president of a large maritime stevedoring and agency company based in Fort Lauderdale. Recommended by the firm's then current president, Arthur Erb, a friend of mine going back to my days at Grace Line, I went through the normal interview process and was eventually offered the position by the owners. My decision to leave Lugo and Navieras was not made lightly. Roberto had gone out of his way to create a job for me when I first called on him, and I owed him a debt of gratitude for that. However, the uncertainty of Navieras's future concerned me a great deal, while the new offer came from a well-established firm with an excellent reputation. The scale tipped in favor of security, and with reluctance I resigned from Navieras and separated from my colleagues and good friends, taking many fond memories with me.

SHIPPING

Resignation of Navieras executive made official

Arthur Novacek moves to Eller & Company in Florida; Lugo D'Acosta will fill the breach effective June 17

By ROBERT RIVAS
CARIBBEAN BUSINESS Staff Reporter

Arthur C. Novacek is as anonymous to the general public in Puerto Rico as he is powerful in the small, intimate group of island shipping company executives.

file precisely because PRMMI is submerged in the highly visible Puerto Rico Maritime Shipping Authority, the legal name for Navieras.

Novacek has been with PRMMI since 1981. Prior to that, he spent five years as president of Moram Agencies Inc., the U.S. marketing arm of the

I am in regular touch with Roberto Lugo to this day, and even on occasion see Robertito, who is the managing vice president in Puerto Rico for Crowley Maritime's steamship container service. Roberto Senior went on to earn his law degree at age 67 from the University of Puerto Rico. Governor Carlos Romero-Barcelo lost the election in 1984, and not long after that, Roberto Lugo and the other senior executives were swept out of Navieras by the new administration. Once again, I was one step ahead.

*   *   *   *

POSTSCRIPT

On March 5, 1995, Navieras de Puerto Rico was sold, due in great measure to losses totaling close to $375 million.* The buyer was the Holt Group, Inc., a Philadelphia-based marine terminal operator and international logistics service provider. In April, 2002, Jacksonville, Florida-based Sea Star Line received U.S. Bankruptcy Court approval of its takeover of Navieras/NPR Inc., part of the Holt Group, which was operating under Chapter 11 bankruptcy protection. The sale of the Navieras/NPR assets and certain related entities was consummated at an estimated price of $32 million. **

* Source: *WELCOME TO PUERTO RICO* website, www.welcometopuertorico.org
**Source: *WORLD CARGO NEWS*, April 2002.

INDEX